NELSON MANDELA

Ann Kramer

RAINTREE
STECK-VAUGHN
PUBLISHERS

A Harcourt Company

Austin   New York
www.raintreesteckvaughn.com

Copyright Permissions
Steck-Vaughn Company
P.O. Box 26015
Austin, TX 78755

Published by Raintree Steck-Vaughn Publishers, an imprint of Steck-Vaughn Company

Library of Congress Cataloging-in-Publication Data

Cataloging-in-publication data is available at the Library of Congress.

ISBN 0-7398-5258-2

Printed in Hong Kong/China. Bound in the United States.

1 2 3 4 5 6 7 8 9 0 LB 05 04 03

Photographic credits
Cover images: Topham Picturepoint

Hulton Archive pp.63, 70
Mayibuye Archives, University of the Western Cape pp. 7, 11t, 18, 41, 47, 65, 73, 75, 76,
Mary Evans Picture Library pp. 26, 33
Popperfoto pp.13,14, 22, 25, 29, 37, 43, 45, 49, 51 (Reuters), 52, 57, 58, 83(Reuters) 84, 87(Reuters), 88, 93, 96 (AFP), 99 (Reuters), 103
Topham Picturepoint pp.2, 3, 4, 11b, 30 (AP), 34 (AP), 61, 66, 79, 81, 95

Nelson Mandela 1918–

Contents

Introduction

"The struggle is my life. I will continue fighting for freedom until the end of my days."

Nelson Mandela was one of the greatest and most influential figures of the 20th century. He led the fight against apartheid (racial separation) in South Africa to become that country's first black president in its first-ever multiracial election.

Nelson Mandela dedicated his life to achieving freedom for his people. His vision was of a democratic South Africa where everyone would have equal rights. Despite many setbacks, Mandela never faltered in his fight to achieve that goal. He spent 27 long years in prison for his beliefs, yet when he was finally released, he astounded the world by his lack of bitterness and his wish to forgive and be reconciled.

Mandela is a man of enormous moral integrity. In court and in prison, his dignity and refusal to compromise his principles won him respect not only from others in the liberation movement but also from his harshest opponents. From ordinary Africans to Afrikaner prison wardens and heads of state, Mandela made friends wherever he went.

In 1993 Nelson Mandela was awarded the Nobel Peace Prize in recognition of his long struggle to end apartheid in South Africa. This was a fitting tribute to a remarkable man respected throughout the world today for his dignity, courage, and tolerance.

▶ *Nelson Mandela is photographed after his release from prison.*

Early Years

Nelson Mandela was born on July 18, 1918 in a tiny village called Mvezo. Mvezo is located in the district of Umtata, in the Transkei region of South Africa.

Mandela's father, Gadla Henry Mphakanyiswa, named his son Rolihlahla, which literally means "pulling the branch of a tree." It can also mean "troublemaker." Mandela's family were Xhosa people. They were members of the Madiba clan, named after a Thembu tribal chief of the 1700s. Mandela's great-grandfather had been a Thembu king called Ngubengcuka. Although Rolihlahla was not a direct descendant, he was nevertheless connected to the royal family. His father was an important and highly respected man in the village and principal adviser to the acting Thembu chief. Gadla had four wives and 13 children. His third wife, Nosekeni Nkedama, was Rolihlahla's mother.

Although an important man in his own right, Mandela's father was subject to the authority of British administrators who had governed the region since 1885. When Mandela was very young, his father quarreled with a white magistrate and was dismissed from his post, losing both his wealth and his wages. Mandela and his mother had to leave Mvezo to live with relatives in Qunu, a small village about 20 miles (32 kilometers) away.

Qunu

Mandela spent his early childhood in Qunu surrounded by an extended family of aunts, uncles, and cousins. The village lay in a small valley and consisted of a

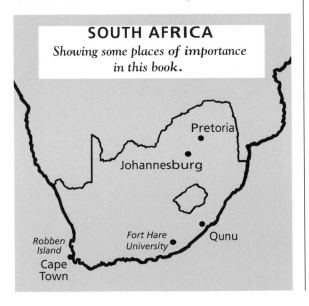

SOUTH AFRICA
Showing some places of importance in this book.

Pretoria

Johannesburg

Robben Island

Cape Town

Fort Hare University

Qunu

settlement of round huts with conical roofs. He and his mother lived in one of the huts. They slept on the floor and cooked over an open fire. Rolihlahla had a traditional and happy country childhood and throughout his life never lost his love for the area.

The region was dependent on cattle, and by the age of five Rolihlahla was a herd boy, looking after the animals as well as playing games such as stick-fighting with the other children. His upbringing

▲ *This conical hut was Nelson Mandela's childhood home in Qunu.*

was strict. His father, who visited regularly, demanded absolute obedience to tradition and custom.

When Rolihlahla was about seven, he was baptized into the Christian faith. He was a clever child and his father sent him to a local mission school, one of many that had been set up by British missionaries to "civilize" Africans and convert them to Christianity. He was the first in his family to go to school. Until now Rolihlahla had always worn a traditional blanket, wrapped around one shoulder and tied at the waist, but for school his father gave him a pair of his own trousers, cut down to size. The schoolchildren were not allowed to keep their African names; on his first day, Rolihlahla's teacher gave him the first name "Nelson."

Royal guardian

Two years later Nelson's father died of lung disease, and Nelson's life changed dramatically. His mother could not afford to continue his education. However, because of her son's ties with the Thembu royal family, Nelson went to live with a wealthy and powerful relative, Chief Jongintaba Dalinyebo, who was acting chief of the Thembu people. Jongintaba became Nelson's guardian and welcomed him into the royal household. He brought up Nelson on equal terms with his own son Justice.

Life was exciting in the royal residence in Mqhekezweni, which was the capital of Thembuland. Although the British ruled South Africa, Jongintaba still had an influential role in the administration of the region, particularly in tribal matters.

Huge meetings were held regularly at the royal palace. People came from all over Thembuland, bringing disputes over cattle and other matters before the chief. Mandela was fascinated by the way Jongintaba and his councillors listened to everyone's opinion before making a decision. This method of resolving conflicts was to influence Mandela's own leadership style later in his life.

Nelson also began to develop a greater awareness of African history and his own culture. Within the royal household, he heard elders tell stories of Africa before the Europeans arrived and of Xhosa resistance to European domination. These stories fired his imagination. He also heard tales of the infamous Robben Island prison and learned about the exploits of many Xhosa and Zulu heroes.

When Nelson was 16 he was circumcised in a traditional ritual that marked his transition from child to adult. During the celebrations afterwards, one of the chiefs spoke forcefully about how the Europeans had destroyed Xhosa culture. Nelson was indignant. He had met very few white people and had always considered them benefactors. In later life,

Mandela believed something was stirred in him that day. This feeling was to flourish and to influence his political future.

Education

Another powerful influence on the young Nelson Mandela was the Christian church. He attended Sunday school and went to a local missionary primary school, where he studied English, Xhosa, history, and geography. A serious, respectful boy, he did well at school, gaining the nickname "Tatomkhulu," which means "Grandpa." Mandela's career had already been decided. His guardian intended that he should continue his education, advancing through the missionary school system until he was ready to become an adviser to the Thembu rulers, thus following in his father's footsteps.

Following primary school, Mandela was sent to Clarkebury, a missionary boarding school about 60 miles (96 kilometers) away, which Jongintaba's son Justice attended. Wearing his first pair of boots, he arrived driven by Jongintaba himself.

Clarkebury was the most advanced educational establishment in Thembuland. It had been founded in 1875 and was a secondary school as well as a teacher training college. From there, at the age of 19, Mandela went to Healdtown, a Methodist boarding school. The school was staffed almost entirely by British teachers and had a harsh routine based on the model of an English boarding school.

Mandela adapted well to his new school. He took up long-distance running and boxing, became a student monitor, and went on to college. He said later, "The education I received was a British education, in which British ideas, British culture, and British institutions were assumed to be superior. There was no such thing as African culture. Whites were unable or unwilling to pronounce an African name and considered it uncivilized."

Student politics

In 1939, 21 years old and dressed in his first suit bought by Jongintaba, Mandela enrolled as a student at the University College of Fort Hare to study for a Bachelor of Arts (B.A.). Fort Hare was an educational institute that accepted high-achieving Africans. Mandela, fresh from the country, found it sophisticated and overwhelming. His cousin, Kaizer

Growing up on the veld

Originally, the Xhosa (the name refers to both the people and their language) lived in the foothills of the Drakensburg Mountains. They moved to the eastern Cape in the mid-1500s and formed clans or family groups, including the Madiba.

Talking of his childhood in Qunu, Mandela said: "It was in the fields that I learned how to knock birds out of the sky with a slingshot, to gather wild honey and fruits and edible roots, to drink warm, sweet milk straight from the udders of a cow, to swim in the clear, cold streams, and to catch fish with twine and sharpened bits of wire. From these days I date my love of the veld, of open spaces, the simple beauties of nature."

compromise was reached. The principal suspended him for the summer and stated that if Mandela reversed his position, he would be allowed to return to Fort Hare and continue his studies.

However, Mandela never returned to Fort Hare. During the summer holidays he learned that his guardian, according to tradition, had arranged marriages for him and Justice. Both young men were unhappy about the arrangements and decided to run away to Johannesburg.

Metanzima, was already a student there. Another student, with whom he would form a life-long friendship, was Oliver Tambo.

Mandela studied English, anthropology, politics, and native administration, and also became involved in student politics. He was elected to the Students' Representative Committee, but resigned as part of a protest against poor diet and inadequate student representation. Despite being threatened with expulsion, which he knew would anger his guardian, Mandela stuck to his principles and a

A university for all

Set up in 1916 by enlightened white liberals and elite Africans, Fort Hare is one of Africa's oldest universities. It was a starting point for many who would go on to become leaders of the liberation movement, including not only Mandela but also Oliver Tambo, Govan Mbeki, and Desmond Tutu.

◀ *Nelson Mandela, about age 21, appears in his first suit.*

▼ *Fort Hare is one of Africa's oldest universities. Many leaders of the liberation movement were educated here.*

Johannesburg

Mandela arrived in Johannesburg in 1940. It was the largest city in South Africa. Mandela, who had never been to a city before, found the cars, bustling streets, and huge buildings immensely exciting.

Mandela and Justice went to the Crown mines in search of work. The power of his father's name instantly landed Justice a job. He also obtained a job as night watchman for Mandela. However, Chief Jongintaba soon learned what they had done and demanded their return, and as a result, both young men lost their new jobs.

Unemployed and with no money, Mandela found lodgings with a cousin, Garlick Mbekeni. Mandela had now decided to complete his degree by correspondence and train as a lawyer.

It might have been an impossible ambition, but fortunately he met Walter Sisulu, who was to become a lifelong friend and comrade in the struggle against apartheid. Sisulu was six years older than Mandela and also came from the Transkei. He ran an estate agency for Africans and was an important community leader.

Sisulu was impressed by Mandela's seriousness and royal connections and introduced him to Lazar Sidelsky, an enlightened Jewish white lawyer. It was rare for an African to work for a white law firm, but Sidelsky offered to take Mandela on as a clerk while he finished his B.A. and then to article (apprentice) him. Sidelsky even waived the premium (cost of training).

Living in Alexandra

Mandela started work at the age of 23 with Witkin, Sidelsky, and Eidelman, one of the largest law firms in the city. The firm handled casework for blacks as well as whites. He rented a room in Alexandra, which was known locally as "Dark City" because there was no electricity. It was overcrowded and the streets were unpaved and dirty. Gangsters

▶ *Walter Sisulu was a lifelong friend of Mandela.*

known as *tsotsis* roamed the township and illegal drinking dens called *shebeens* were common. Nevertheless, Mandela found living in Alexandra exhilarating.

During the day, Mandela worked at the law firm as a clerk and messenger, filing documents and delivering papers around Johannesburg. He earned a weekly salary of £2 ($1.30), barely enough for basic needs. At night, he studied by candlelight to complete his B.A. He often went hungry and walked the six miles (nine kilometers) to and from work to save money. Sidelsky even gave Mandela an old suit, which he stitched and patched up and wore almost every day for five years.

Every Sunday his landlord provided Mandela with lunch, which was his only hot meal of the week. During his time in Alexandra, Mandela also learned the realities of poverty and experienced racism firsthand.

Friends and political allies

Mandela was making friends and being slowly drawn into politics, despite warnings from Sidelsky. At the office he became

◀ *Conditions for black Africans in the townships were grim, as in this picture of Alexandra township.*

friendly with the only other African employee, Gaur Radebe , a communist who had helped launch the African Mineworkers' Union in 1941. Mandela also befriended Nat Bregman, another articled clerk in the firm and also a communist. Bregman invited Mandela to parties, where he found himself mixing with Africans, whites, Coloureds, and Indians, most of whom were communists. Mandela was becoming increasingly aware of the racial oppression in his country, but for him communism did not seem to provide an answer.

Witwatersrand University

In 1942 Mandela passed the final exam of his B.A. The following year he enrolled as a part-time law student at the University of Witwatersrand, one of only four English-speaking universities that allowed high-achieving blacks to attend specialist courses. Mandela was the only black student on the law faculty.

"Wits," as the university was known, opened up a new world of ideas and political beliefs for Mandela. At the university he met white and Indian people of his own age. Many of these were radical intellectuals who welcomed

Mandela into their circle. Among them were people who would later work with him in the liberation struggle. They included Joe Slovo, an ardent communist; Ruth First, a left-wing activist who later married Slovo; George Bizos, an important legal mind; Bram Fischer, a part-time lecturer; Ismail Meer, a key member of the Indian National Congress; and many others.

Political beginnings

In August 1943 Mandela had his first taste of direct protest when he marched with Gaur and others in support of a bus boycott. This was sparked when bus fares from Alexandra to central Johannesburg were raised. In protest some 20,000 Africans boycotted the bus service, walking to work instead. Protesters blocked the roads, the buses traveled empty and within nine days the bus owners backed down and reinstated the original fares. Mandela found the experience of marching with his people inspiring and was also impressed by the effectiveness of the boycott.

Encouraged by Sisulu, in 1942 Mandela joined the African National Congress (ANC), a black organization founded in 1912 to improve conditions for Africans. Sisulu's house was a meeting place for ANC members. Oliver Tambo was often there, as was Anton Lembede, an African nationalist.

Lembede believed Africans had to lose their respect for western ideas and need for white approval. By reclaiming their own culture, they could break free of oppression. His views strongly affected Mandela, who knew he was in danger of becoming one of the African elite approved of by the British and criticized by Lembede.

Youth League

Mandela and his colleagues in the ANC believed that the organization was out of touch with most Africans. They decided

Mobilizing African youth

The ANC Youth League's manifesto stated: "The national liberation of Africans will be achieved by Africans themselves." It rejected white control and European "trusteeship," whereby Europeans argued that their governments had African interests at heart. It called for the repeal of all anti-African legislation, criticized the ANC for its failures, and called upon African youth to push for change.

to form a Youth League to transform the ANC into a mass movement against white oppression.

First, however, the ANC had to approve, and a delegation that included Mandela went to see Dr. Xuma, the ANC president. He was opposed to their views and suggested the League should act as a recruiting agency for the ANC, saying that Africans were too disorganized to take part in mass campaigning.

On this basis the ANC's annual conference accepted the League. In September 1944 it was formally launched with Lembede as president, Tambo as secretary, and Sisulu as treasurer. Mandela was elected to the executive committee. Together with his colleagues he produced the League's manifesto, and in 1947 he was appointed secretary.

Marriage and family

Life was not all work and politics. At Sisulu's house Mandela also met a trainee nurse, Evelyn Mase, and they married in 1944. They rented a house at 8115 Orlando West (later to become part of Soweto township). It had a tin roof, a cement floor, a tiny kitchen, and a bucket toilet and was to be Mandela's home for

Living in Johannesburg

Originally a mining town, Johannesburg was founded during the gold rush of 1886. When Mandela arrived, it was a vast sprawling city. The wealthy white population lived in expensive villas. Africans, however, lived in squalid, overcrowded quarters in "non-European townships," such as Alexandra, Sophiatown, and the Western Native Township. Alexandra was one of the few places where blacks could buy land or property.

Hundreds of Africans arrived in Johannesburg every week seeking work. They were treated as temporary residents and had to carry "passbooks" showing written permission to live and work in the city. A color bar existed, which meant that black Africans could not enter hotels and restaurants. Most Africans were restricted to poorly paid manual work.

Mandela remembers: "I cannot pinpoint a moment when I became politicized, when I knew that I would spend my life in the liberation struggle. To be an African in South Africa means that one is politicized from the moment of one's birth. A steady accumulation of a thousand slights, a thousand indignities, and a thousand unremembered moments produced in me an anger, a rebelliousness, a desire to fight the system that imprisoned my people."

many years. Their first child was born, a son named Madiba Thembekile, who was nicknamed "Thembi." Mandela was rarely at home, but he enjoyed playing with Thembi, bathing him, feeding him, and reading him stories. A year later they had a second child, a daughter named Makaziwe, who died when she was only nine months old.

Influential events

In 1947 Mandela was three years into his apprenticeship. The couple were dependent on Evelyn's earnings as a nurse, but important events were shaping Mandela's political development. In 1946 African mineworkers went on strike in the biggest labor protest to date in South Africa. The strike was brutally crushed. Mandela gave his support to the strike and through it met J. B. Marks, an influential communist.

The Indian community also began a mass protest against repressive legislation that restricted their right to purchase land. The campaign lasted until 1948, and many of the leaders, including Ismail

Meer, went to prison. Their defiance impressed Mandela. In 1948 the white National Party won the national general elections and formed the new government of South Africa. Their first move was to establish apartheid. From now on Mandela became wholly dedicated to the struggle for freedom.

◀ *Mandela and his first wife, Evelyn, pose for a photograph.*

European Dominance

Although apartheid became official policy in 1948, its origins lay in a long history of European exploitation of Africans that stretched back 300 years.

Under apartheid, black South Africans were taught that their history began with the arrival of the Europeans. But, as Mandela learned, it really began thousands of years before.

The earliest peoples of what is now South Africa were hunter-gatherers known as Khoisan, who moved into the region about 10,000 years ago. Gradually they became cattle herders and moved southwards into the Cape area to find new grazing lands.

In about 300 A.D., Bantu-speaking peoples from central Africa also arrived. They established settled communities, growing crops, herding cattle, and mining metals such as iron. Over generations different tribal communities evolved, including the Swazi, Xhosa, and Zulu. Chiefs and royal houses ruled the different tribes.

The Dutch arrive

The first European settlers arrived in the region in 1652 when a party of Dutch colonists, led by Jan van Riebeeck, established Cape Town, a trading post at the Cape of Good Hope. Initially a stopping point for ships of the Dutch East India Company traveling between Europe and Asia, it soon grew into a larger colony. More Dutch settlers arrived, who called themselves Boers (farmers) and later Afrikaners.

Relations between the Europeans and native Africans were unequal from the start, and the Dutch treated the Africans with disdain. Initially they bought cattle from the Africans, but the Khoisan were reluctant to part with their livestock, so

▶ *A map of South Africa circa 1900 demonstrates European control of the region.*

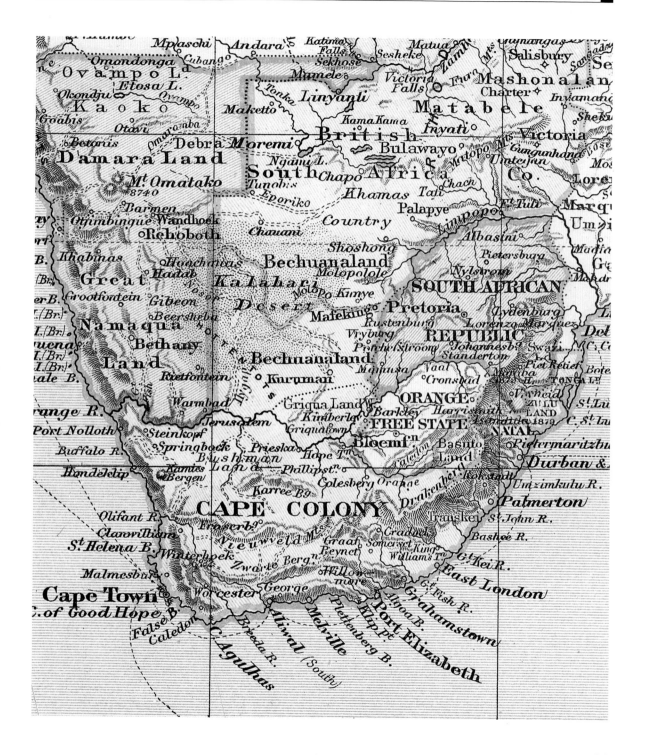

the Dutch began to forcibly seize their grazing lands and cattle.

The Khoisan defended their lands but their bows and spears were of little use against the Europeans' superior weapons. Bands of Khoisan raided Dutch farms. Before long the Boers were organizing commando forces to seize back livestock, but they also slaughtered African men, women, and children, with official approval from Dutch administrators who regarded the Africans as "vermin." By the end of the 1700s, the Khoisan had been virtually exterminated. Survivors were captured and forced to work for the Boers. There was some intermarriage between Dutch and Africans. This resulted in mixed-race descendants known as "Cape Coloureds."

By this time Xhosa people had moved southward, where they first encountered the Dutch. In 1779 the first of a series of wars broke out between the Boers and Xhosa. The wars continued for the next 20 years, but the Dutch were unable to subdue the Xhosa.

◀ *An early photograph of Boers trekking to the interior of Africa in covered wagons.*

British control

In 1806 the British, who also had trading interests in Asia, seized Cape Colony. From 1811 they waged a military campaign against the Xhosa, destroying crops and villages. Throughout the 1800s the British army fought various African peoples, forcing them to submit to imperial rule. The British defeated the Xhosa and fought the Zulus, overpowering them at the Battle of Blood (Ncome) River in 1838 and AmaQonqo in 1840.

The Great Trek

By 1828 the Boers, who believed they were God's chosen people, owned nearly 6,000 African slaves. Some of these were taken from the Xhosa and some were imported from elsewhere on the continent. This situation was embarrassing for the British, who in 1833 banned slavery. British administrators declared there should be equal rights in Cape Colony, but this never really happened.

In 1836 about 6,000 Boer men, women, and children left Cape Colony, driving northward in wagons across the Orange and Vaal rivers in what became known as the Great Trek. They established two independent Boer republics, the Transvaal

(1852) and the Orange Free State (1854). Both were based on the idea that black Africans were inferior to whites.

The Boers had also trekked into Natal, but in 1843 it was annexed by Britain. A secretariat of native affairs and separate "reserves" for blacks were established. After 1849 Africans were subjected to a so-called "hut tax," whereby they had to rent land and homes from white colonists. This forced Africans into the position of having to work for the white settlers. Beginning in the 1870s, the Boers and the British carried out a further series of campaigns against various African peoples.

Gold and diamonds

In 1868 diamonds were discovered in the Transvaal Republic and nearly 20 years later gold was found in the Orange Free State. These discoveries led to even greater European control over the African population. Prospectors poured into the region and the prospect of huge wealth attracted European imperialists such as Cecil Rhodes, eager to stake a claim for themselves.

Dispossessed of their own land, thousands of Africans were forced to find work in the mines. Most became migrant laborers who left rural areas and their families searching for work. European employers insisted that Africans should carry written passes and labor certificates giving them permission to work in the mines. African miners were forced to live in barrack-style compounds, in specially created black-only locations. Thus migrant labor became a feature of apartheid.

Anglo-Boer Wars

The enormous mineral wealth intensified rivalry between the Boers and the British. In 1880–1881 the Boers successfully fought the British to retain Transvaal's independence. However, following the South African or Boer War (1899–1902), Britain seized the Orange Free State, occupied Johannesburg, and annexed Transvaal. The Boers fought a bitter guerrilla war to preserve their independence but were ultimately defeated. The British promised better conditions for Africans; at least 10,000 Africans had fought on the British side against the Boers, but their optimism was

▶ *Boer guerrillas pose with their weapons, c. 1900.*

misplaced. After the war, Boer farmers returned, and displaced any Africans who had reclaimed their lands.

By 1900 most of South Africa was in European hands. In 1906 the Zulu chief Bambatha led the final armed African rebellion against British rule. It was brutally suppressed, and 4,000 Africans died.

Union of South Africa

In 1910 the British colonies of the Cape and Natal merged with the former Boer republics of Transvaal and the Orange Free State to form the Union of South Africa, a British dominion. The four provinces could decide on their own allocation of political rights. In Transvaal and the Orange Free State, black Africans had no political rights at all. Only white men could vote or become members of parliament. In Natal, Africans, Indians, or Coloureds who satisfied certain economic conditions could vote, although few did. Only in Cape Colony could men of any racial group vote, provided they were literate

◀ By the time this young Zulu warrior was photographed in about 1900, many Africans had lost their lands and were forced to work for colonial employers.

and owned property. In reality, the majority African population had virtually no rights in the new Union.

Boers and Zulus

Dutch farmers in South Africa called themselves Boers or Trekboers from the Dutch *boer,* meaning farmer, and *trek* meaning to pull (a wagon). Later, they called themselves Afrikaners, after the Afrikaans language they developed, which was a simplified form of Dutch combined with some Portuguese and African words.

The Zulus were skilled warriors who lived in the northeast province of Natal. From 1818 until his death in 1828, Shaka, a great Zulu chief, united many Nguni tribes to create a Zulu nation. The Zulus resisted both the Boers and the British for many years. Under their leader Cetshwayo (r. 1873–84), Zulu warriors won many important battles against the British. In 1879, armed only with shields and spears, they defeated the British army, killing 1,800 British soldiers. Their final rebellion, led by Chief Bambatha, came in 1906.

Mandela recalls: "At Mquekezweni I learned of African heroes like Sekhukhune, king of the Bapedi, the Basotho king, Moshoeshoe, and Dingane, king of the Zulus, and others such as Bambatha, Hintsa and Makana, Montshiwa and Kgama … I discovered the great African patriots who fought against Western domination."

From Union to Apartheid

On May 31, 1910, the Union of South Africa came into being as a self-governing country within the British Empire. The population numbered some 5.9 million, of whom 4 million were black African, 500,000 were Coloureds, and about 150,000 were Indian.

Only about 1.3 million (about 25 percent) of the South African population were white, either Afrikaans- or English-speaking, but this minority held all the power. Black people were entirely excluded from parliament; in 1936 their limited voting rights were removed.

Africans who had supported the British during the Boer War had hoped British rule would mean more rights, but soon after the Union was formed, new and repressive laws were introduced that only strengthened the control of the colonial government.

The Land Acts

In 1913 the Natives Land Act was passed. This prohibited black Africans from buying land in all but a small percentage of territory, known as reserves, which were set aside for them. Under apartheid, these reserves would form the basis of so-called Bantustans or "homelands."

Africans who had previously rented land from Europeans were driven onto reserves where sustainable farming was impossible, and forced to work for white bosses. They also needed passes or written permission to move from one region to another. A second Land Act in 1936 reinforced the situation, leaving the white minority legally "owning" 87 percent of the country.

During World War I (1914–18), industry in South Africa boomed, and

▶ *Symbol of white oppression: Shown here is the magistrate's court at Umtata, capital of Transkei. Transkei was the first Bantustan (area reserved for black Africans) created by the government in 1927.*

many Africans went to the cities in search of work. Afraid of what was perceived as a black invasion, the government passed the 1923 Natives (Urban Areas) Act. This act controlled the number of black people arriving in urban centers and forced them to live in specific areas, effectively creating segregation.

African resistance

In 1912 the African National Congress (ANC) was formed to oppose the forthcoming Natives Land Act. Initially, it was called the South African Native National Congress (SANNC). The founders, an elite group of Africans educated through the same missionary school system that Mandela later experienced, did not challenge white rule but wanted white rulers to recognize African rights.

Early ANC leaders kept a belief in British justice and used peaceful law-abiding tactics of persuasion, sending delegates and petitions to London to argue their case. Their efforts were unsuccessful.

◀ A "Whites Only" sign in English, Afrikaans, and Bantu stood at a South African beachfront.

As the black labor force grew, some Africans began to organize into trade unions. In 1921, when Mandela was three years old, the South African Communist Party was formed. Initially it recruited white members only, but from 1925 it also recruited black workers, building up a large black membership.

In 1920, 71,000 African gold miners struck for better pay and conditions. The strike was put down brutally by soldiers and police. Eleven miners were killed and more than 100 injured. Even so, black resistance grew steadily, and in 1928–29 communists called for black majority rule and closer cooperation with the ANC.

White-only governments

Throughout the first half of the 20th century, a succession of white-only governments ruled South Africa; however, tension continued between Afrikaners and the British.

The British dominated the economy and enjoyed far greater wealth than the Afrikaners, who made up 60 percent of the white population. In spite of their lesser wealth, Afrikaners tended to be the most important political force.

There were two main political groups: the pro-Afrikaner National Party founded in 1914 by General Herzog, which promoted the interests of Afrikaners, and the pro-British South African Party led by General Jan Smuts, which ruled South Africa from 1910 to 1924.

In 1924 Afrikaner nationalists gained power when the National Party joined with the smaller Labour Party to form a coalition government. It increased South African independence from Britain and protected the rights of white workers against black workers. Conditions for African workers deteriorated and, as black resistance grew, government policies became more hardline. The issue of so-called "native policy" began to dominate South African politics.

Rise of the National Party

In 1934, with unemployment on the rise, the National Party merged with the South African Party to form the United Party. This was led by Jan Smuts, a pro-British Boer who had been prime minister between 1919 and 1924. Later the same year, an extreme group of Afrikaner nationalists, who sympathized with Adolf Hitler's German Nazi Party and its racist policies, formed a new National Party under Daniel F. Malan, a former Dutch Reform minister. This party became the official parliamentary opposition and used racial anxieties to gain support for its policies.

World War II

Under Smuts' leadership, South Africa joined World War II (1939-45) on the British side. The economy boomed again and the number of black workers grew. Many moved into towns and some restrictions on them were eased. Black political activity also increased. It was at this time that Mandela arrived in Johannesburg, joined the ANC, and helped to form the Youth League. Restrictions on blacks were lifted during the war and many Africans hoped that Smuts would introduce further reforms; however, this was not to be.

Nationalist victory

Exploiting the ruling minority's fears of *swart gevaar* (the "black danger") and fighting the election on a slogan *Die kaffir op sy plek* ("The nigger in his place"),

▶ *South African leader Jan Smuts (1870–1950) is photographed in dress uniform.*

Malan's National Party won the 1948 election.

The night before the election, Mandela had been at an all-night political meeting. When he emerged in the morning to see the newspaper headlines announcing the nationalist victory he was "stunned and dismayed." He later commented, "From the moment of the nationalists' election we knew that our land would henceforth be a place of tension and strife." He and his colleagues had assumed that Smuts, then very popular, would soon return to power. Mandela had little faith in Smuts, but he knew that Malan's extreme views would make things much worse.

Apartheid

The National Party government, which would control South Africa for more than 40 years, believed in white supremacy. It began reshaping the country by introducing apartheid, an Afrikaans word meaning "apartness" or "separateness." New laws were passed formalizing the oppression of the previous years.

Among other things, the new laws classified the peoples of South Africa into four so-called "racial groups": whites, Coloreds, Indians, and Africans. Mixed marriages were banned and Africans and other racial groups were to be completely separated from whites in every area of life. Beginning in 1948 notices saying "Whites Only" or "Nonwhites Only" began appearing in all public places including beaches, lavatories, buses, trains, theaters hotels, and restaurants. The government also moved to stamp out any opposition, banning the Communist Party and recruiting more police and soldiers to enforce its policies.

Apartheid laws

- 1949: Prohibition of mixed marriages between different racial groups.
- 1949: Immorality Act makes sexual relations between different racial groups illegal.
- 1950: Population Registration Act labels South Africans by race.
- 1950: Group Areas Act sets up different urban areas for each racial group.
- 1950: Suppression of Communism Act bans the Communist Party of South Africa. Also used to silence any opposition to the government.
- 1953: Reservation of Separate Amenities Act prohibits people of different colors or racial groups from mixing in all public areas from transport to beaches.

◀ *Johannesburg resident Timothy Mayisela displays the passbook that all blacks had to carry with them to prove they were allowed in white areas of the town.*

Defiance

Mandela and the ANC Youth League (ANCYL) had spent four years trying to radicalize the ANC. Now, shocked by the 1948 election results, there was no more time to waste.

Immediately after the election, Mandela and other ANCYL leaders including Sisulu, Tambo, Peter Mda and James Njongwe, drew up a program of action for a mass movement against apartheid. It was to be based on nonviolent civil disobedience and would make use of boycotts, strikes, demonstrations, and passive resistance.

Once again Mandela went to see the ANC president, Dr. Xuma, who rejected the proposals, describing Mandela and his friends as "naive firebrands." At the 1949 ANC annual conference, however, the older, more conservative leaders were replaced. A more militant president was chosen, Sisulu was elected secretary general, and Tambo was voted to the executive committee.

As a result the ANC made nonviolent civil disobedience its official policy. It was a triumph for the Youth League and, as Mandela noted, he and his colleagues had now graduated to the senior organization.

In 1950 Mandela was elected to the national executive committee of the ANC.

Protest and repression

The ANC called for a nationwide day of protest against the government's racist policies. At about the same time, a Defend Free Speech Convention was organized by the Transvaal ANC, the Transvaal Indian Congress, the African People's Organization, and the Communist Party.

The convention attracted 10,000 people in Johannesburg and there were calls for a general strike on May 1, 1950. Mandela supported the aims but felt Africans should organize for themselves. He was also wary of communists taking over the liberation movement.

▶ *The May 1 protest day was followed by many others throughout the 1950s. Here, nonwhites gather in Johannesburg in 1952 to protest against apartheid.*

Mass protest grew and so too did government repression. The dangers of protest became clear in 1950 when mounted police fired on unarmed protesters in Orlando West, killing 18 Africans. Mandela witnessed the event.

The same year the Suppression of Communism Act outlawed the Communist Party, making it a crime to be a party member. The act was also used to suppress antiapartheid activists. Laws were also passed restricting Indian and Colored rights. A thoughtful man, Mandela changed his views at this point. He realized that all nonwhite groups were under threat; from now on the liberation struggle had to be multiracial. The ANC remained an all-black organization, but from this point its policy was to work with other groups.

Despite a ban on political meetings, the ANC's national day of protest went ahead on May 1, 1950. Mandela coordinated plans at the ANC office. The ANC's first nationwide strike was a moderate success. Most urban black workers stayed at home and businesses did not open. Mandela found his first significant role in a national campaign an exciting experience.

Defiance Campaign

In 1952 the ANC, supported by other groups, launched a Defiance Campaign Against Unjust Laws. Small groups of trained volunteers would begin to defy the apartheid laws by deliberately entering whites-only areas without passes and getting themselves arrested. The organizers hoped this would snowball into mass defiance.

Mandela was national volunteer-in-chief. He organized the campaign and recruited, trained, and coordinated volunteers. He had recently passed his driving test and drove around the country talking to potential volunteers, explaining the issues and warning them of the dangers. He stressed the importance of nonviolence, believing the authorities would come down hard on any aggressive behavior.

Four days before the campaign began, there was a mass rally in Durban. Mandela was the main speaker at the meeting. Addressing a crowd of 10,000 people, Mandela told them they were about to make history. The Defiance Campaign would focus the world's attention on the racist policies of South Africa and its leaders.

The campaign was launched on June 26, 1952—the ANC's Freedom Day—when 33 volunteers in Port Elizabeth walked through the whites-only entrance to the railroad station and were arrested. In Johannesburg, 52 protestors, with Sisulu and Nana Sita of the Indian Congress at their head, were also arrested. That evening Mandela was arrested and taken to Marshall Street police station with 50 others. They entered the cells singing *Nkosi Sikelel' iAfrika* ("God Bless Africa"), the African national anthem and rallying cry of resistance that Mandela describes as "hauntingly beautiful."

At the police station, a white police officer pushed a volunteer, breaking his ankle. When Mandela protested, the officer kicked him. Mandela spent two days in prison before being released on bail.

Results and reaction

The Defiance Campaign lasted six months, spreading throughout urban areas and into the countryside. Some 8,000 volunteers were arrested, without having committed a single act of violence. The government reacted ruthlessly, raiding ANC offices and

Fighting for freedom

Looking back at this period of the struggle, Mandela said:
"The [Defiance] campaign freed me from any lingering sense of doubt and inferiority I might still have felt; it liberated me from the feeling of being overwhelmed by the power and seeming invincibility of the white man and his institutions. But now the white man had felt the power of my punches and I could walk upright like a man, and look everyone in the eye with the dignity that comes from not having succumbed to oppression and fear. I had come of age as a freedom fighter."

introducing even more repressive laws. Mandela was arrested again, charged under the Suppression of Communism Act, and sentenced to nine months' imprisonment, suspended for two years. A massive demonstration took place when he appeared in court.

The laws were not repealed, but for Mandela the campaign was successful. The government had seen that defiance existed and opponents of apartheid were prepared to go to prison for their views. Starting with the Defiance Campaign, going to prison became a badge of honor among Africans, and ANC membership soared to 100,000.

Banned

At the ANC's annual conference in 1952, a new president, Chief Luthuli, was elected. Mandela became president of the Youth League and the Transvaal ANC, but he could not attend the conference in person. A few days earlier he had been put under a banning order, a new government measure that prohibited him from leaving Johannesburg or attending any meetings for six months. He could not even attend his son's birthday party.

It was the first of many bans he would experience. Mandela felt "banning was a dangerous game, for one was not shackled or chained behind bars; the bars were laws and regulations that could easily be violated and often were. One could slip away unseen for short periods of time and have the temporary illusion of freedom."

Marriage problems

Mandela's second son, Makgatho Lewanika, was born in 1950. Although Mandela was with Evelyn for the birth, politics and work meant he was spending less and less time at home. Another daughter, Makaziwe, was born in 1953. But by the mid-1950s the marriage was in difficulty. According to Mandela,

Evelyn never accepted his political commitments, but the reality was that he had probably fallen out of love with Evelyn. Soon they were living separate lives.

Mandela and Tambo

Mandela was also working full-time. He had passed his law degree and, having worked for various enlightened law firms, decided to set up his own practice. Oliver Tambo worked nearby in Johannesburg and the two often met for lunch. Never one to miss a political opportunity, Mandela always waited for Tambo in the whites-only waiting room.

In 1952 they went into partnership. Their firm, Mandela and Tambo, was the first black law firm in South Africa. It provided a much-needed legal service for ordinary Africans. Every morning Africans crowded into their small waiting room, many having fallen foul of the apartheid system with its confusing pass, curfew, residence, and employment laws.

▶ *Oliver Tambo (left) is pictured with Nelson Mandela.*

Mandela was in and out of court all day long. Every case was a reminder of how badly Africans were treated under apartheid. All judges were white, but Mandela refused to be intimidated by the racism often directed toward him. One magistrate was so resentful that he demanded to see Mandela's certificate before proceeding. White witnesses refused to answer Mandela's questions and police witnesses treated him with contempt. In response, Mandela behaved as if the court belonged to him, often employing a flamboyant courtroom style.

Under apartheid law, Mandela and Tambo's offices were illegal. The authorities refused to renew their permit, insisting they move the practice to a township some miles away. They defied the law and so remained under constant threat of eviction. In 1954 the Transvaal Law Society petitioned the Supreme Court to have Mandela struck off (removed from the register of lawyers) because of his political activities. Surprisingly, the Supreme Court turned down the petition and levied costs against the society.

Despite these problems the law firm prospered, and for the first time in his life Mandela was relatively wealthy. He bought an Oldsmobile car and fashionable suits. More than 6 feet (1.8 meters) tall, he was a dramatic figure who exuded confidence and energy.

Under police scrutiny

The police kept Mandela under constant surveillance. Everything he did and everyone he spoke to was written down and permanently recorded in police files.

Mandela believed it was only a matter of time before the ANC was declared illegal, so he drew up measures known as the "M-plan" that could allow the ANC to operate as an underground, or secret, organization when the time came. His idea was to split the organization into a network of smaller units, or cells.

In 1953 the government announced its intention to forcibly remove more than 60,000 Africans from Sophiatown, a freehold township in Johannesburg, to a tract of land known as Meadowlands. The ANC was determined to resist the removals and Mandela, his banning order

▶ *Tension in South Africa rose dramatically during the 1950s, and many feared civil war was not far away. Nevertheless, protests remained nonviolent, as here in Johannesburg.*

having expired, spoke at various public meetings mobilizing support. On one occasion, he drew attention to heavily armed police, who were standing around taking notes. As he spoke Mandela became angry and said passive resistance would not defeat a minority government determined to retain power at any cost.

His words appalled the ANC leadership and he was reprimanded. He accepted the rebuke. The police, however, became more and more repressive. Mandela was served with another banning order, requiring him to resign from the ANC leadership, restricting him to Johannesburg, and prohibiting him from attending meetings or gatherings for a period of two years.

Secretly Mandela continued to play an important role in the antiremoval campaign and also in protests against the government's Bantu education policy. The ANC was unable to prevent the Sophiatown removal or maintain a boycott against the use of so-called Bantu schools (see sidebar), and by 1954 momentum seemed to be running out. The ANC therefore decided to call a national convention, a move that would bring together all opposition groups to

Apartheid education

The 1953 Bantu Education Act applied apartheid to education. Schools for Africans, which had been run by the church or missions, were to be taken over by the state to provide an education designed specifically to make Africans "realize that equality with Europeans is not for them."

If these so-called Bantu schools did not abide by the act, they would lose the limited funding they received. For Africans who could not afford to pay for private education, this meant their children either received an inferior education or no education at all.

plan a program for a democratic South Africa. It was to be a major landmark in the antiapartheid movement and would have far-reaching consequences.

▶ *Angry antiapartheid protesters give the ANC "thumbs-up" salute as they sing* Mayi Buye Afrika, Kose Sikalara *("May we, Africa, arise").*

Treason

In 1955 a Congress of the People met at Kliptown, near Johannesburg. More than 3,000 delegates braved police intimidation to draw up a "Freedom Charter."

Mandela and Sisulu, who were both under banning orders, stood at the edge of the crowd to avoid being seen. The congress lasted two days during which each clause of the charter was read aloud in English, Sesotho, and Xhosa, debated on, and settled. Toward the end of the second day, armed police and Special Branch detectives broke up the congress. The crowd remained peaceful, singing protest songs as each delegate left after giving his or her name to the police.

The Freedom Charter affirmed the right of all South Africans, regardless of race, to vote, hold office, and be equal before the law. Mandela said it was "a beacon for the liberation struggle" and a blueprint for a democratic, multiracial South Africa. He never deviated from its principles. The first lines of the charter read: "We, the people of South Africa, declare for all our country and the world to know that South Africa belongs to all who live in it, black and white, and that no government can justly claim authority unless it is based on the will of the people; that our people have been robbed of their birthright to land, liberty, and peace by a form of government founded on injustice and inequality."

Government backlash

The government, which saw the Charter as a revolutionary document, reacted with more repressive measures. Just before dawn on December 5, 1956, police raided Mandela's house. As his children watched, he was driven away to the Marshall Square prison. More arrests took place, with police arresting 156 people in all, including most of the ANC leaders.

▶ *A 1956 photograph shows all 156 Treason Trial defendants.*

TREASON TRIAL

The ACCUSED

DECEMBER 1956

For two weeks they were held in the Fort, Johannesburg's chief prison. Mandela and the other nonwhite activists, a total of 120 people, were locked in two prison cells. They slept on cement floors with three thin blankets and one open lavatory in each cell. They refused to be intimidated and their cell became a kind of convention for freedom fighters, somewhere they could discuss politics and sing freedom songs. Under apartheid, white activists were placed in a separate area.

Treason Trial

All 156 prisoners were charged with high treason and conspiracy to overthrow the government in order to set up a communist state. The penalty for treason was death. The prosecution cited the Freedom Charter, the Defiance Campaign, and other events as proof.

The trial opened on December 19, 1956. The accused traveled to court in a convoy of police vehicles, with supporters cheering and waving along the route. As Mandela said, their trip from the jail to the court became a "triumphal procession." On the second day, 500 armed police surrounded the court and the prisoners were put into a wire cage. The cage, however, was dismantled later following protests.

The prosecution took two days to read the charges before the accused were released on bail. Supporters set up a defense fund to help them. Mandela had to report to the police every week and be available to attend court at great cost and disruption to his legal practice, family life, and political work.

The trial dragged on for more than four years, and despite the gravity of the charges, Mandela noticed that it sometimes descended into farce. The prosecution presented 12,000 documents, including police notes, ANC pamphlets, the Universal Declaration of Human Rights, and even a Russian cook book. One hundred and fifty state witnesses gave evidence, much of it false. Discrepancies and lies were exposed by a defense team that included Bram Fischer (see p. 16) and Vernon Berrangé.

In 1957 charges against 61 of the accused, including Luthuli and Tambo, were dropped for no reason. In 1958 the

▶ *A group of African sympathizers outside the Treason Trial courthouse give the ANC salute. The man second from right wears an ANC badge.*

The Freedom Charter

Laid down in the Freedom Charter was a set of principles for a multiracial democratic South Africa. About 200 organizations including white, black, Indian, and Coloured were invited to send in suggestions. Circulars were sent to townships and villages, inviting people to put forward their suggestions. The most common demand was for one person, one vote. When drawn up, the main points included:
• Democracy and the right to vote for all South Africans, whatever their color
• Redistribution of land and wealth
• Equal rights in law
• The right to work, housing, security, peace, and friendship

trial was moved to Pretoria, a two-hour daily bus ride away, making life more difficult for the accused and moving them away from their supporters. Charges were suspended against another 65 defendants, leaving 30, including Mandela, to return to court.

In 1960 Mandela finally took the stand. Confident and at ease in the witness box, he was pleased to have the chance to present his answers to people who wanted to prove that he was a violent communist. During his testimony, he reaffirmed the ANC's commitment to nonviolence and its demand for political rights for all. He said he was not a communist but emphasized the help communists had given.

In 1961 the trial collapsed. The judge said there was evidence of illegal activities, that the ANC was trying to replace the government, but there was no evidence to prove the ANC or its Freedom Charter advocated violent communist revolution. All the accused were found not guilty and discharged.

It was a humiliating defeat for the government; they had failed, and Mandela had emerged as an impressive figure. The trial had provided a rallying point for the antiapartheid movement.

Divorce and remarriage

In 1956, while Mandela was in prison, his marriage broke up and Evelyn moved out of their home, taking the children. In 1958 they divorced. The breakup upset the children, particularly Thembi, then age ten. Mandela was close to his eldest son and they enjoyed boxing and jogging together. For a while they were alienated.

▶ *Nelson and Winnie Mandela pose for a wedding photo in May 1958.*

In 1957, age 38, Mandela met Nomzamo Winifred Madikizela, known as Winnie. She was 22 and a social worker. Mandela was struck by Winnie's beauty and immediately fell in love with her. They married in 1958. The trial was still underway and Mandela, under a banning order, needed special permission to leave Johannesburg for six days. Their bridal car was covered in the ANC colors of green, yellow, and black.

Mandela and Winnie were a striking couple. They were happy together, but their married life was fragmented. Mandela was either attending the trial, involved in political activities, or trying to keep his law firm from collapsing, which it finally did. Only rarely could

▲ *In the aftermath of Sharpeville, armed South African police move among dead bodies. At least 69 people were killed and more than 180 injured.*

they spend time together, going out to eat a curry, Mandela's favorite food, or listen to jazz. Even then, people were always approaching Mandela and wanting to talk to him. Their home at 8115 Orlando West was comfortable, but police raids were constant.

Winnie supported Mandela's political beliefs. She joined the ANC's Women's League and became involved in the struggle. In 1959 their first daughter Zenani, known as "Zeni," was born. In 1960 they had a second daughter, Zindiziswa, who was nicknamed "Zindzi."

Grand apartheid

In the late 1950s, apartheid was extended into what became known as "grand apartheid." It became a crime for blacks to attend church services in white areas without written permission, and the pass laws were extended to women. In 1958 Hendrik Verwoerd became prime minister. His aim was nothing less than total racial segregation.

The Promotion of Bantu Self-Government Bill was passed, providing for the establishment of black homelands (Bantustans). Mandela described the bill as a "crude, empty fraud." Ostensibly, it seemed to allow Africans the right of self-government in their own areas; in fact, it exacerbated tribal tensions and kept black Africans subjugated and in poverty.

The Sharpeville massacre

Opposition to apartheid grew, and many Africans were inspired by liberation movements happening elsewhere on the continent. Ghana obtained independence from Britain in 1957; other African countries followed in the 1960s.

In 1959 a new group, the Pan African Congress (PAC) broke away from the ANC. The PAC was headed by Robert Sobukwe, one of Mandela's friends. It was an African nationalist organization and a rival to the ANC. The PAC called for a mass protest against the extended pass laws, which came into force by 1960.

Several thousand demonstrators gathered outside the police station in Sharpeville. Police opened fire on the crowd, which turned and fled. At least 69 Africans were killed and 186 were wounded, most of them shot in the back as they ran away. The same day, police used nightsticks to break up a crowd in Langa, killing two people and injuring 49 others.

The Sharpeville massacre made front-page news throughout the world and highlighted the increasing viciousness of apartheid. Protest became worldwide.

ANC banned

After Sharpeville, Mandela and his colleagues called for a national strike and day of mourning. Mandela publicly burned his pass in front of the world's press, as did many other freedom fighters. Thousands turned out for the strike and the day of mourning.

Despite international pressure—Britain, the United States, and the UN Security Council condemned the shootings at Sharpeville—the South African government refused to budge, and Verwoerd ordered a huge crackdown. A state of emergency was declared and the ANC, together with the PAC and other antiapartheid organizations, was declared illegal.

Mandela in prison

Hundreds of activists were rounded up and arrested. Tambo was smuggled over the border; others escaped into exile. The police raided Mandela's house and arrested him without a warrant. He was taken to the police station, where he found Sisulu and others.

The men were packed into a small, open yard where they spent the night without food or blankets. The following morning they were put in a tiny cell. The only toilet was a single drainage hole in the floor, which soon became blocked. They had no food until the afternoon and were eventually given mats to sleep on and blankets encrusted with vomit and blood. Mandela, who was ordered to take his hands out of his pockets, was so furious he nearly came to blows with the station commander.

Mandela was moved to a prison cell in Pretoria, where he was held for five months. He attended the trial from prison. In prison, Mandela shared a cell with four others. They had one toilet bucket, which was emptied once a day. The air was foul, the blankets riddled with lice, and for the first ten days the prisoners were not allowed to shower or exercise.

Mandela, as spokesman, engaged with the authorities in a constant struggle for better conditions, even taking his complaints to the courtroom. As a result of his negotiations, the cells were cleaned, the men were given new blankets and toilet buckets, and Mandela won the right to use an area for legal consultations.

Moving underground

In August 1960 Mandela was released from prison and, although banned, could finally return home. At a secret meeting, he and others made plans for the ANC to operate as an underground organization along the lines of the M-plan they had devised in 1952.

Mandela's banning order was due to expire on March 27, 1961, and final judgement in the Treason Trial (which had begun on December 19, 1956) was to follow two days later. The ANC decided that if the accused were acquitted, Mandela would go into hiding and lead underground operations, surfacing in public at carefully planned occasions to get maximum publicity.

All-in Africa Conference

On March 25, 1961, Mandela appeared at an All-in Africa Conference in Pietermaritzburg. He addressed 1,400 delegates. Mandela had not been seen on a public platform for nearly five years and his arrival had been kept secret. In an electrifying speech, he challenged the apartheid regime to call a national convention of all South Africans to devise a new constitution for a democratic, integrated country. South Africa was about to become an independent republic free of British control, and he warned that failure to call the convention would lead to a mass general strike to coincide with independence. He also wrote to Verwoerd but received no reply.

On March 29 the defendants in the Treason Trial were acquitted, amid massive celebrations. Instead of joining them, Mandela immediately went underground.

Underground

Soon after the Treason Trial ended, a warrant was issued for Mandela's arrest as the only identified member of the national action committee organizing the mass strike.

If caught, Mandela was certain to go to prison. He decided to avoid capture, go into hiding, and continue organizing the strike. To pass unrecognized, he grew a beard and wore overalls, disguising himself as a gardener or, with a cap, as a chauffeur. This was particularly effective because he could drive a car under the guise of being a black "boy" working for a white master.

Mandela stayed on the move as the police hunted him everywhere. He traveled secretly around the country, moving at night from one safe house to another and drumming up support for the mass strike. The police set up roadblocks throughout the country, but were unable to catch him. He had some narrow escapes. On one occasion a chief of secret police drove up alongside his car but failed to recognize him. On another occasion, an African policeman did recognize him, but secretly gave the ANC sign and went on his way. Mandela was pleased.

Every so often there were reports that he had been seen, and from time to time he phoned in stories to the press. His exploits delighted the people and he was nicknamed "the Black Pimpernel," after a fictional character called the Scarlet Pimpernel who always avoided capture.

Strike

The national strike was planned for May 29–31, 1961, to coincide with South Africa becoming a republic. In response, the government mounted its largest show of strength to date. The army was called out, military units were placed outside townships, tanks were moved in, and police numbers were increased.

Despite the dangers, on May 29, thousands of people, Coloured workers, including Indians and Africans, stayed home and refused to go to work. The strike overshadowed the Republic Day

▶ *This picture of Mandela was taken sometime before he was jailed in 1964.*

celebration but was not as large as Mandela had hoped, and he called off the action on the second day.

New tactics

Mandela thought new tactics were needed. It was evident the government was prepared to use maximum force to crush the antiapartheid movement, and in his view nonviolence was not going to change its attitude. Instead, he believed that in the face of government intimidation, armed struggle was the only option left. He knew that following so soon after the Treason Trial, it was going to be a sensitive issue with the ANC leadership, but he believed it to be the right way.

In June Mandela had a secret meeting with various ANC executive members in Tongaat, a small village north of Durban, near Chief Luthuli's home. Mandela explained his views, arguing that the state had given them no choice and that violence was already occurring with or without the ANC initiating it. The following night there was a second

◀ *Walter Sisulu burns a passbook in 1960. Soon he and Mandela were to abandon such low-key acts for more direct action including sabotage.*

meeting with people from other organizations, including the Indian Congress, the Colored People's Congress, and the South African Congress of Trade Unions. Once again Mandela put forward the case for armed struggle.

The meeting lasted all night. Some disagreed with Mandela, including Chief Luthuli and many Indian leaders, but after hours of discussion, a decision was reached. The ANC would remain committed to its policy of nonviolence, but if Mandela wanted to set up a military organization, the ANC would not stand in his way.

"Spear of the Nation"

Mandela was authorized to set up a separate organization not subject to ANC control, and to recruit and enlist the help of whomever he needed. The new organization was called *Umkhonto we Sizwe* (Spear of the Nation), or MK. Its high command consisted of Mandela as commander, Joe Slovo as chief of staff, and Walter Sisulu.

They began to recruit activists and prepared to carry out acts of sabotage against selected targets, such as power stations and communications centers. Their intention was not to kill people but to damage the state. They also needed to prepare themselves for possible armed struggle or guerrilla warfare.

There were difficulties, not least the fact that Mandela and his colleagues had no military experience (Mandela had never even fired a gun). Through Slovo, Umkhonto enlisted help from white Communist Party members who had been operating underground for some years. They also recruited Jack Hodgson, a former soldier who taught them the details of bomb-making. He was their first demolition expert. They practiced setting off explosions in an old brick works, with Mandela attending the first attempt.

Mandela always believed in educating himself and read as much as he could on guerrilla warfare, including writings by the revolutionaries Che Guevara, Mao Zedong, and Fidel Castro, as well as Karl von Clausewitz's classic work on war.

Rivonia

In October Mandela moved to Liliesleaf Farm in the Rivonia area near Johannesburg. It was owned by sympathetic whites, and Mandela, who took the name David Motsamayi, pretended to be the houseboy or caretaker. Raymond Mhlaba, one of Umkhonto's first recruits, and later Slovo and Rusty Bernstein, another arms expert, joined him for a while. Among them, they wrote Umkhonto's constitution. Planning meetings were also held at the farm.

For a while it was a peaceful sanctuary. Winnie and the children were able to visit and they often spent weekends with him. Mandela said: "We were secure, however briefly, in this idyllic bubble."

One day, when Mandela was listening to the radio, he heard that Chief Luthuli had been awarded the Nobel Peace Prize. Mandela was pleased. It showed that the West recognized their struggle. It was also a slap in the face for the National Party. However, the timing was awkward, as Umkhonto was just about to begin their sabotage campaign.

Sabotage

On December 16, 1961, Umkhonto carried out its first acts of sabotage when homemade bombs exploded at electric power stations and government offices in Johannesburg, Port Elizabeth, and

▶ *Chief Luthuli opposed outright violence, but agreed not to interfere with Umkhonto's activities.*

Durban. One Umkhonto recruit was accidently killed, but otherwise there was no loss of life. Thousands of leaflets were distributed simultaneously around the country, announcing the existence of Umkhonto and taking responsibility for the bombings.

The government was taken completely by surprise. White South Africans were shocked as they realized their lives were not as secure as they imagined. Two weeks later, a second wave of explosions occurred.

A fugitive abroad

Three weeks after the sabotage campaign began, Mandela left South Africa. The ANC had been invited to attend a conference of the Pan-African Freedom Movement for East, Central and Southern Africa (PAFMECSA) in Addis Ababa, Ethiopia, and the ANC decided that Mandela should go. He would also seek help for the struggle.

On January 11, 1962, Mandela left South Africa for the first time in his life. He was driven to Bechuanaland (today's Botswana) then flew to Tanganyika (present-day Tanzania). Waiting in a hotel, Mandela noticed whites and blacks sitting together on the veranda. He had never been in a public place where there was no color bar and he realized that for the first time he was in a country governed by Africans. He later said, "Though I was a fugitive and wanted in my own land, I felt the burden of oppression lifting from my shoulders."

Mandela met with Tambo, who had left South Africa in 1960 and had already set up ANC offices in Ghana, England, Egypt, and Tanganyika. In February 1962 he addressed the conference in Addis Ababa, describing their struggle and asking for help. From Ethiopia, Mandela went to Egypt, Tunisia, Morocco, Guinea, Sierra Leone, Liberia, Ghana, and Senegal, meeting important leaders and gaining support in the form of money, military training, or arms. To his disappointment he learned that some Africans regarded the PAC, with its strictly African nationalist stance, more sympathetically than the ANC, and were critical of the ANC's multiracial stand.

In June 1962 Mandela went to London for ten days. He operated in secret, not wanting information to leak back to

▶ *Mandela poses for a photograph outside Westminster Abbey in London, 1962.*

South Africa. Nevertheless, he met with some politicians and supporters and went sightseeing with Tambo. Mandela loathed imperialism, but admired the British parliamentary system and many aspects of the British way of life. He visited the Houses of Parliament and Westminster Abbey, and took a boat trip on the Thames River.

From Britain, Mandela returned to Ethiopia to be trained in guerrilla warfare. He learned how to use an automatic rifle and a pistol and learned how to make small bombs and mines. If a guerrilla war began, he wanted to fight with his people.

After eight weeks he received a message from Sisulu in Johannesburg insisting he return to South Africa where conditions were becoming increasingly violent. The sabotage campaign had continued and in response the government had introduced a new antisabotage act. Violation of the act now carried the death penalty, and the government was clamping down hard. Mandela was needed at home.

Rivonia Trial

Posing as a chauffeur, Mandela crossed back into South Africa with Cecil Williams, a white MK member. They arrived in Liliesleaf Farm where Mandela immediately met with Sisulu, Kotane, Govan Mbeki and others. From there, despite Mbeki's warning that it was too dangerous, Mandela went to Durban for further meetings.

On August 5, 1962, Williams and Mandela drove back to Johannesburg. A car filled with white men shot past them. Looking around, Mandela saw two other cars, also full of white men. He knew "my life on the run was over; my seventeen months of 'freedom' were about to end."

A police officer produced a warrant for Mandela's arrest, and although Mandela gave his false name, the police knew exactly who he was. Mandela was taken to Marshall Square police station where he was put into a solitary cell.

Charged

On August 7 Mandela appeared in court. He was charged with leaving the country illegally and inciting African workers to strike. With relief he realized there was no evidence to charge him with sabotage.

Winnie and Slovo were in the court and there were hundreds of supporters outside. When he emerged to enter a sealed van destined for the Fort prison, they greeted him with a popular ANC political call and response, shouting *Amandla* ("Power"), followed by *Ngawethu* ("The Power is Ours"). His arrest was headline news.

Detained

Mandela was detained pending trial and kept in isolation in the most secure area of the prison. The ANC and Umkhonto worked out escape plans, but Mandela felt they were not practical and wrote a note to Slovo saying the plans should be postponed until he was convicted. He asked Slovo to destroy the note, but it was kept as a historical document and later used in court.

▶ *This photograph of Mandela was taken at the time of the Rivonia Trial in 1963.*

Visitors came to the prison, including Winnie, who brought him pajamas and a silk dressing gown—unsuitable for a prisoner, but a sign of solidarity. They discussed the possibility of a long imprisonment and how she would manage on her own with the children. At one point he was taken to prison in Pretoria, where visiting was more restricted. While awaiting trial, Mandela exercised daily and began studying for a further law qualification.

Sentenced

The court case began on October 15, 1962. The ANC had set up a "Free Mandela" committee and there were countrywide protests. The slogan "Free Mandela" began to appear on the sides of buildings. The committee also organized a mass demonstration for the court case.

Mandela entered a packed court wearing a traditional Xhosa leopardskin kaross (robe) to make the point that he was a black man entering a white man's court. His supporters roared approval, raising their arms and clenching their fists in support. Winnie, sitting in court, was also dressed in traditional clothing. The prosecution called more than 100 witnesses from all over South Africa.

The charges against Mandela were indisputable and there was no point in his pleading not guilty. Instead, Mandela dispensed with counsel and witnesses and used the court as a showcase for his beliefs and to denounce the government. He spoke for an hour, explaining how and

Protesters outside the courthouse demand the release of the ANC leaders.

why he had become a freedom fighter and how, ultimately, he had to choose between compliance with the law, which was "immoral, unjust, and intolerable," and accommodating his conscience. He finished by saying that posterity would pronounce him innocent and the criminals who should have been in court were the government.

He was sentenced to five years' imprisonment, the harshest sentence imposed to date in South Africa for political offenses.

In prison

Once in prison, Mandela was stripped and ordered to put on prison uniform— short trousers, rough khaki shirt, canvas jacket, socks, sandals, and cloth cap. Racism existed in prison as elsewhere. Only blacks were made to wear short trousers because Africans were treated as "boys" by the authorities. Their food was also the worst in prison.

Mandela refused to wear the shorts or eat the food and was put into solitary confinement. He had no watch, nothing to read, and no one to talk to. It was profoundly dehumanizing, and he says at times he found himself "initiating conversations with a cockroach."

After some weeks Mandela demanded to be put with the other political prisoners, and ultimately he was moved out of solitary. In May 1963 he was suddenly moved to Robben Island, the maximum security prison built on a rocky outcrop about 18 miles (28 kilometers) off the coast of Cape Town. After some time he was moved back to Pretoria. The authorities said this was for his own safety because he had been threatened by PAC political prisoners. This was completely untrue.

Charged with sabotage

In July 1963, while serving his sentence, Mandela was charged with a further offense, this time of sabotage. The police had raided Liliesleaf Farm, catching almost the entire Umkhonto high command and seizing hundreds of documents. One was entitled "Operation Mayibuye," and it contained draft plans for guerrilla warfare in South Africa.

On October 9, 1963, Mandela and 10 co-accused were taken in a heavily fortified van to the Supreme Court in

Pretoria. Their trial, which became known as the Rivonia Trial, was to be the most significant trial in apartheid history.

Security was intense; police armed with machine guns surrounded the court. The accused entered flanked by armed guards. Mandela was dressed in prison clothes and had lost weight, but he smiled at the supporters and made a clenched fist ANC salute.

Mandela and his comrades were formally accused of sabotage and conspiracy to commit sabotage. They had already been warned that, if found guilty, they were likely to be executed. They fully expected this to be the case.

The course of the trial

The prosecution's case began in December. It set out to prove not only sabotage, but also that Umkhonto was part of the ANC and that guerrilla warfare existed and was accepted ANC policy. The state produced 173 witnesses, thousands of documents and maps, plus a sketched map of the Fort and even the note that Mandela had written postponing the escape plans. The cornerstone of the state's case was the six-page plan of action, which had been drafted when Mandela was abroad.

While the trial continued, Mandela and his fellow accused met in prison to discuss and plan their defense. It was not easy since their cells were bugged and they were watched constantly, which meant they had to pass notes to each other and destroy them immediately.

The defense team included Bram Fischer. Since Fischer had been involved in underground work this was a huge risk for him. Other members of the team were Bizos and Berrangé. Bit by bit they undermined aspects of the indictment, proving the ANC and Umkhonto were separate organizations and that guerrilla warfare had not begun.

Mandela knew there was plenty of evidence to convict him, including

Penalties for sabotage

Between 1962 and 1963 South Africa became a virtual police state. Under a so-called 90-day detention act, anyone suspected of political activity could be detained for an indefinite period and without a warrant. ANC and PAC members were rounded up and imprisoned; many of them were tortured. Beatings, electric shocks, suffocation and other forms of torture were used widely, and in 1963 the first detainee died in prison.

documents in his own handwriting. He and his codefendants had decided not to deny the charges but to use the trial as a propaganda outlet. In court, they intended publicly to admit responsibility and to explain their political beliefs and why they had resorted to violence. During the trial the defense lawyer Joel Joffe said: "He [Mandela] had no concern for his own position. His aim was to turn the trial into a showcase against the government."

On April 20, 1964, under the tightest security Pretoria had ever seen and with his mother and Winnie in court, Mandela took the stand. He had prepared a detailed statement, which he read aloud. It took four hours to read. He admitted he was one of the people who helped to form Umkhonto we Sizwe and explained his reasons for doing so. He stressed the difference between the ANC and Umkhonto, described his own political beliefs, outlined conditions for black Africans under apartheid, and finished with his commitment to the struggle. When he finished, the court was absolutely silent. Despite the ban on printing, his speech was published in the local and international press.

Conclusion and reaction

In May the prosecution concluded its case. It was garbled and, according to Mandela, even the judge seemed mystified. By this stage it had become clear that the judge had already accepted two key points: that guerrilla warfare had not begun, and that the ANC and Umkhonto were two separate organizations.

By now the trial was receiving worldwide attention. The U.S. Congress, the Soviet prime minister and international trade unions had protested. British M.P.s (members of Parliament) had staged a protest march and night-long vigils in support of the accused were being held outside St. Paul's Cathedral in London. The UN Security Council had

Mandela's ideals

The final part of Mandela's closing speech at the Rivonia Trial on June 12, 1964: "During my lifetime I have dedicated myself to the struggle of the African people. I have fought against white domination and I have fought against black domination. I have cherished the ideal of a democratic and free society in which all persons live together in harmony and with equal opportunities. It is an ideal which I hope to live for and achieve. But if need be it is an ideal for which I am prepared to die."

urged South Africa to end the trial and grant amnesty to the defendants.

Life imprisonment

On June 11, 1964 the judge returned the verdict. Mandela and his colleagues knew most of them would be found guilty. Despite the threat of execution, they had decided not to appeal, prepared to become martyrs to the cause. The judge found them guilty but did not impose the death sentence. Instead seven of the accused were sentenced to life imprisonment. The crowd gasped in relief. Mandela smiled at his comrades, looked around for his mother and Winnie, and was taken down to the cells.

Rivonia Seven

Seven of the accused in the Rivonia Trial were sentenced to life imprisonment on Robben Island. They were: Nelson Mandela, Walter Sisulu, Govan Mbeki, Ahmed Kathrada, Raymond Mhlaba, Andrew Mlangeni, and Elias Motsoaledi.

◀ *This photograph of Mandela was taken in 1964, just before he was sentenced to life imprisonment.*

Robben Island

Within hours of the trial, Mandela and his comrades were flown to Robben Island, site of what Mandela described as "the harshest, most iron-fisted outpost in the Southern African penal system." Mandela was 46; he would not be free again for 27 years.

The authorities had built a special maximum security area within the prison to house Mandela and the political prisoners, isolating them from others. It was a one-storey rectangular stone fortress surrounding a flat courtyard. There were cells on three of the four sides; the fourth side was a high wall with a catwalk patrolled by guards with dogs.

The prisoners were put in individual cells. Mandela's cell overlooked the courtyard. It had a small eye-level window and was only about 6 feet (1.8 meters) wide. Mandela could walk its length in three paces; when he lay down, his feet touched one wall and his head grazed the other. On his cell door was a white card bearing his name and prison number, 466/64. The walls were about 2 feet (0.6 meters) thick and constantly damp. When Mandela complained about the damp, he was told his skin would eventually absorb the moisture. For bedding he had three worn blankets and a sisal mat. A bucket in the cell was the only toilet.

Category D

Racism was a fact of life. All guards were white; many were brutal. Torture was common and prisoners were beaten with whips, canes, and hose. They were punished for the smallest infringement of rules, often by being put in solitary confinement. Guards insisted on being called *baas* (boss) and they called prisoners *kaffirs* (niggers). African prisoners were forced to wear the hated short trousers, received worse food than other prisoners, and had to tip their caps to wardens and guards.

Mandela, like the other political prisoners, was a category D prisoner, which meant he had minimum privileges.

▲ *Prison conditions were grim at Robben Island.*

He was allowed only one visit and one letter every six months and no study privileges. He was not allowed a watch or clock. Almost immediately, he made a calendar to keep track of time.

Hard labor

A morning bell woke Mandela at 5:30 A.M. He was not allowed out immediately, so used the time to stretch and take whatever exercise was possible in his tiny, cramped cell. At 6:45 A.M., he was let out to clean his toilet bucket.

He then returned to his cell for a meagre breakfast of cold corn mash. Inspection followed and if he failed to tip his cap, he would be put into solitary confinement.

From the cell he was taken to the courtyard, where he and the others sat crosslegged on the ground. In front of each prisoner was a pile of stones. Forbidden to talk, they hammered the stones into fine gravel. Lunch was boiled corn and a corn and yeast drink, followed by half an hour of supervised exercise. Stonebreaking continued for some hours. Mandela washed under a seawater shower, returning to his cell at 4:00 P.M. Supper was maize porridge and at 8:00 P.M. the prisoners were ordered to sleep, with a light burning in the cells all night.

After six months pounding stones in the prison courtyard, Mandela and his colleagues were sent to work in the lime quarry. Conditions were appalling—the work was heavy and the glaring light was painful. It was three years before they were allowed sunglasses, and even then they had to pay for them. A warden told Mandela they would work for only six months in the quarry; in fact, it was 13 years. At least in the quarry the prisoners had some opportunity to talk, and

Mandela enjoyed the daily walk to and from the site.

Challenging the system

Locked away from the outside world, Mandela knew it would be easy to be crushed, but refused to give way to despair. An optimist, he maintained his dignity and his determination, always believing one day he would leave prison. He felt a new struggle had begun and that by improving conditions on Robben Island, he was continuing to challenge apartheid. Survival depended on solidarity with his comrades and he later said, "By sharing we multiplied whatever courage we had individually."

He believed the authorities made a mistake putting the political prisoners together; they gained strength from each other and so managed to survive.

Mandela refused to be cowed by the harsh prison regime. He challenged everything, demanding better food, better clothes, study privileges, and an end to the discrimination shown to African prisoners. He refused to call the guards *baas* and eventually the issue was dropped. When stonecrushing quotas were raised, Mandela and his comrades refused to meet them, and again their

▲ *Mandela (left) and Walter Sisulu talk in prison.*

determination overcame the demand. Mandela considered courtesy and dignity the best strategies, even with the guards, and gradually won the respect of many in the prison. He learned to keep his emotions tightly under control and rarely lost his temper. With these traits he soon became spokesman and leader.

When official visitors came to the prison, such as the International Red Cross, it was Mandela who voiced complaints on behalf of other prisoners. Gradually, and with many setbacks, he began to win concessions.

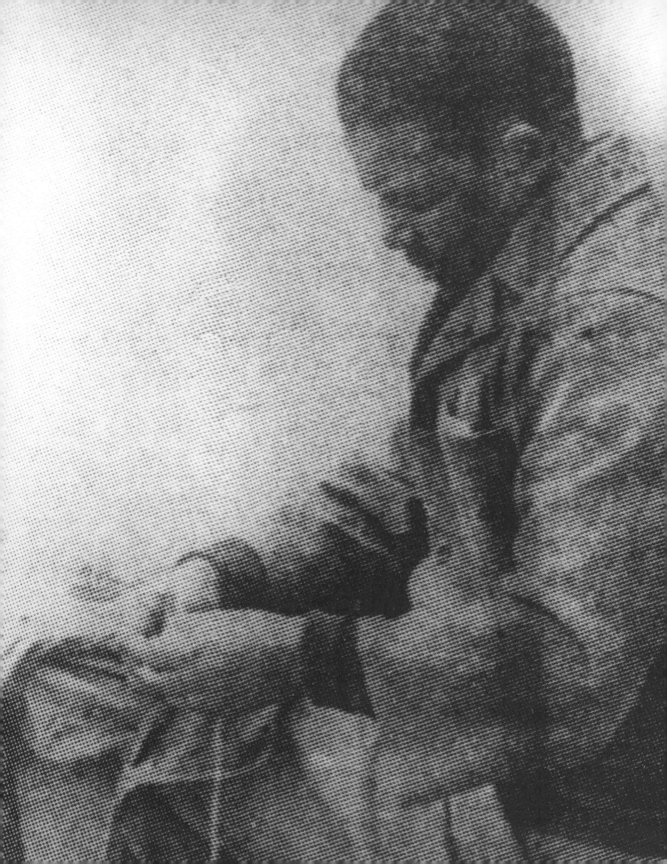

◀ *This photograph shows Mandela sewing a mailbag while in prison on Robben Island.*

Keeping in touch

Communication inside prison and with the outside world was difficult and often dangerous. Talking was usually prohibited, newspapers and radios were forbidden, and letters were heavily censored, sometimes with whole chunks cut out.

Mandela and his comrades found ingenious methods of communicating. They wrote miniscule notes, passing them through the prison network, hidden in matchboxes or taped inside toilet buckets. Sometimes newspaper cuttings found their way into prison. The punishment for reading a newspaper was solitary confinement, something that Mandela was already experiencing.

Family tragedies

Mandela longed for contact with his family, particularly Winnie. Letters from her were "like the summer rain that could make even the desert bloom." She visited two months after Mandela arrived on Robben Island and was then put under a banning order and could not visit again for two years. Mandela worried about her. She and their daughters were constantly harassed, and in 1969 she was arrested. The prison authorities made sure Mandela knew by leaving press cuttings in his cell. In Pretoria, Winnie underwent a brutal interrogation for five days and nights and was kept in solitary confinement for six months before being charged. She spent more than 400 days in prison before being released and was then put under a five-year banning order.

In 1968 Mandela's mother died, having made only one visit. He was refused permission to attend her funeral. In 1969 his eldest son Thembi was killed in a car crash. Mandela was devastated and spent all night staring out of his window, with Sisulu trying to offer comfort. Again Mandela was refused permission to attend the funeral.

It was a dark time for Mandela as he questioned his right to put his political struggle before his family's needs. He was powerless to protect his family from persecution and felt guilty about it.

"The university"

By 1966 there were 1,000 political prisoners on Robben Island and the authorities finally granted them study privileges. While the ANC operated in

Robben Island

Robben Island had been a leper colony, naval base, and mental hospital as well as a prison. Mandela was not the first Xhosa to be imprisoned there. In 1819 Makanna (or Nxele), commander of the Xhosa army, was banished there by the British after leading 10,000 warriors against them. He tried to escape by boat, but drowned.

exile outside South Africa, Mandela and his comrades aimed to keep political awareness and the ANC alive in prison. They ran courses and lectures for other political prisoners. At night their cell block was more like a study than a prison; among themselves, they called it "the university." Sisulu lectured on the history of the ANC, while Mandela taught political economy.

Mandela, Sisulu, Mbeki, and Mhlaba formed a high command, with Mandela as leader. They kept in touch with prisoners in the general section and made strategy and policy decisions about how to challenge the prison system and improve conditions. One policy decision, for instance, was that guards who showed respect to prisoners should be given respect in return. This led to arguments with PAC prisoners.

Changing conditions

Under Mandela's leadership, in the 1970s the prisoners won some concessions. They gained three mats and five blankets each to sleep on, and were entitled to two sets of clothing including underwear. They also won the right to one letter and visitor per month and to keep photos in their cells. Mandela immediately put a photograph of Winnie on his cell wall.

In 1973 the lime quarry routine changed when Mandela and the others were given alternative work gathering seaweed. It was bitterly cold on the seashore, but Mandela took pleasure in seeing the Cape Town skyscrapers in the distance. He also relished the chance to make nourishing seafood stews and collect shells for his cell.

Over the years, prison took its toll. Mandela tried to keep fit physically and emotionally, by studying and following a strict daily exercise regime, but by 1975 he had high blood pressure and problems with his back and eyes. He was given a chair because of his back problems and, after many years, won permission to have a garden, which he loved. News about police treatment of Winnie caused him constant anxiety and it was not until

1975 that he finally saw their two daughters for the first time in 12 years. Zeni was 16 and Zindzi was 15. Mandela was 57. He began to write his memoirs, which he and his colleagues planned to have smuggled out of prison for publication on his 60th birthday in 1978. Unfortunately the manuscript was discovered, and Mandela lost study privileges for four years.

▼ *This photograph shows Mandela (left) and two other men working in the garden at Robben Island.*

Prison visiting

Until the mid-1970s, Mandela was allowed only two visitors a year. Visits were limited to 30 minutes and took place in a cramped, windowless room. A thick piece of glass, with holes drilled in it, separated Mandela from any visitors, including Winnie or his children. He could only talk about family matters; any reference to politics was banned. Mandela and Winnie developed a code, based on their family life, to pass information. "I always knew that some day I would once again feel the grass under my feet and walk in the sunshine as a free man."

The Struggle Continues

By 1976 the outside world had all but forgotten Mandela. However, events occurred in South Africa that would bring him back into the center of the political arena.

With Mandela and other activists in prison or in exile, it seemed resistance had been crushed, and the government pushed ahead relentlessly with its policy of separate development. White prosperity increased and nearly 100,000 Africans lost their homes as so-called "black spots" were eliminated. Apartheid seemed immovable, but news of dramatic events began to filter through to Mandela in his prison cell.

Black consciousness

In the early 1970s a new generation of militant black activists emerged. Most were students who had grown up under apartheid and one of their leading spokespersons was a medical student, Steve Biko. They formed the "black consciousness" movement and believed in Africans making changes for themselves, rejecting white-led organizations or white sympathizers.

Biko and other leaders were put under banning orders, but in spite of this, black consciousness spread, partly inspired by liberation movements in Mozambique and Angola, where Portuguese colonial rule had collapsed in 1974.

The Soweto uprising

Black consciousness reached a peak in Soweto. On June 16, 1976 thousands of students and schoolchildren in Soweto staged a mass protest against a government ruling that half their classes should be taught in Afrikaans—for them, the language of the oppressor. Without

▶ *In Soweto, the police opened fire on residents, killing 13-year-old schoolboy Hector Pieterson.*

warning, the police opened fire, killing a 13-year-old schoolboy, Hector Pieterson. Running battles between police and demonstrators continued for three days; at least 150 people were killed, most of them schoolchildren. The killings made headline news around the world, highlighting as never before the brutality of apartheid.

Young lions

Mandela first knew of these events through whispered conversations when, after the Soweto uprising, black consciousness activists were rounded up and imprisoned on Robben Island. Some were put in the isolation unit, where they refused to accept prison rules and were disrespectful of the older political prisoners.

Mandela was impressed by their courage and militancy and called them "young lions." Seeing himself as an elder statesman, he sent notes to the leaders, welcoming them to the prison. He was eager to learn as much as possible about their views and to recruit them into the ANC. There were disagreements, mainly because many of the young activists saw Mandela and his colleagues as old,

middle-class intellectuals, but ultimately many "young lions" joined the ANC.

Changing conditions

Conditions on Robben Island were gradually changing. For 13 years Mandela had demanded an end to hard labor and, in 1975, he and his colleagues went on a "go-slow" protest at the quarry. In 1977 the authorities, hard-pressed by the new influx of political prisoners, finally capitulated and ended hard labor. In 1978 political prisoners were at last allowed to listen to censored news broadcasts, and from 1980 they could buy selected newspapers.

Mandela spent his time reading (he was forbidden to study), preparing legal briefs for other prisoners, gardening, playing tennis, and exercising. Most days he did 100 fingertip pushups, 200 situps, 50 deep knee bends, and ran in place for 45 minutes—a punishing regimen even for a much younger person. He felt isolated and worried that he was being left behind. Some of his prison friends had been released; other old colleagues had died, including Luthuli, Fischer, and Kotane.

▶ *Black consciousness leader Steve Biko is photographed in the early 1970s.*

▲ *While he was ANC president-in-exile, Oliver Tambo gave press conferences abroad. In London in 1976 he called for "drastic action against the South African regime before it is too late."*

Winnie banished

Mandela also worried about Winnie. Living in Soweto, she had been actively involved in the protests, and in 1976 she was detained and imprisoned for five months. The following year, to Mandela's distress, she and their daughter Zindzi were forcibly removed from their home and taken to Brandfort, a remote township some 250 miles (400 kilometers)

southwest of Johannesburg. They and their possessions were dumped in front of a three-room, tin-roofed shack in the bleak township where they knew no one and did not speak the local language.

The police regularly harassed Winnie and Zindzi, who became profoundly depressed. From prison, Mandela managed to get an injunction against the security police to leave Zindzi alone but, as always, he felt powerless.

In 1977 his daughter Zeni married Prince Thumbumuzi, son of the king of Swaziland, an enlightened traditional leader and member of the ANC. A year later she visited Mandela with her husband and their newborn daughter. Mandela was able to hold his new granddaughter, whom he named Ziziwe, meaning "hope."

Free Mandela

Mandela had been virtually forgotten, but there were signs that the antiapartheid movement was gathering momentum. After Soweto there was widespread international condemnation of South Africa. This intensified in 1977, when Biko died in police custody after a vicious beating. Representatives from 13 western governments attended Biko's funeral, and in London and Washington there were demands for economic sanctions against South Africa. In 1977, in protest against apartheid, the Commonwealth formulated the Gleneagles Agreement to discourage South African involvement in sport.

Protests broke out again in South Africa when news came of Biko's death; in 1980 Umkhonto restarted its sabotage campaign. The government outlawed all black consciousness groups, but apartheid was now coming under criticism from some white South Africans. There was a serious shortage of skilled labor, and some of the white business class were beginning to demand an end to restrictive apartheid labor laws that confined blacks to low-skilled employment.

In 1980 the focus switched to Mandela himself. Tambo was ANC president-in-exile, based in Lusaka, Zambia. On his suggestion, the Johannesburg *Sunday Post* started a campaign for Mandela's release under a large headline: "Free Mandela." Under the headline was a petition inviting readers to sign and demand the release of Mandela and his fellow prisoners.

A famous prisoner

Mandela thought no one would remember him, but the campaign was a success with black organizations and white sympathizers, including English-speaking South Africans and some wealthier Afrikaners.

The Free Mandela campaign eventually spread worldwide. Streets and student bars were named after him, songs were written about him and, in 1981, Mandela learned that students at London University had nominated him for the honorary post of chancellor.

In 1980, on the 20th anniversary of Sharpeville, Mandela's daughter Zindzi addressed a huge gathering of white students at Witwatersrand University. In her speech she said that releasing Mandela was the only hope of avoiding bloodshed.

Mandela was now the world's most famous prisoner; his presence on Robben Island was the symbolic focus for the whole antiapartheid movement. In 1982, as calls for his release continued, he was suddenly told to pack his things. Together with Sisulu, Mhlabe, and Mlangeni, he was taken from Robben Island to Pollsmoor Prison on the mainland.

Mandela Freed

Pollsmoor was a maximum security prison a few miles southeast of Cape Town. The Rivonia comrades were kept in isolation on the third floor, away from other prisoners.

Initially, Mandela found the move disorientating. He missed the comradeship and outdoor life of Robben Island, which had been his home for 18 years. There was still no word of release.

Conditions in Pollsmoor were better. Mandela suspected this was the case because the world was watching. The prisoners were held in a spacious room with regular beds and a bathroom. There was also a terrace, where Mandela created a kitchen garden, growing vegetables in cut-down oil drums. He had newspapers and a radio and he was allowed to see his family more often. In 1984 "contact" visits were allowed, and he could touch his wife for the first time in 21 years. However, Mandela's family was still persecuted; Zindzi was beaten up and Winnie's house was gasoline-bombed.

State of emergency

Mandela was now more connected to outside events. In 1981 the South African government had launched a military attack against ANC offices in Maputo, Mozambique, killing 13 ANC members, including women and children. In 1982 they attacked an ANC outpost in Lesotho, killing 42 people. Ruth First, a leading antiapartheid activist and Joe Slovo's wife, was killed by a letter bomb.

In retaliation, Umkhonto stepped up the sabotage campaign. It bombed power stations and a military intelligence office in Pretoria, causing loss of life. Mandela was disturbed by the civilian deaths, but saw them as a consequence of government actions. Tension and violence escalated in the townships; some young blacks turned violently on others, accusing them of being informers.

The government responded with a huge show of strength, and a state of emergency was imposed in the mid-1980s.

▶ *Happy 70th birthday: Supporters in London sign a huge card for Nelson Mandela in 1988.*

Dear UNCLE NELSON
LOVE, PAUL, ADIE, ZOYA
TANYA AND NADIA
Ronnie Dind
Isry Dind
Annabel
Thomas
Christian Greetings
Giles Chesley Harcourt
David Kerr
EDWARD DAVIE
Peggie Preston
DOREEN
Fiona Bettles
Joe Lake
Rosy Wilson
Roger Cornwell
Hannah Stanton
Elaine Fletcher
Jed Davis

United Democratic Front

Increasingly under pressure, in 1983 P. W. Botha, the South African president, made some constitutional changes, including a new three-chamber, or tricameral, parliament that included Coloreds and Indians. He also said he would remove the mixed-marriage ban. When asked about this, Mandela said it was not his intention to marry a white woman or swim in a white pool; that what he wanted was political equality.

In 1983 a number of groups, linked to the ANC in exile, merged to form the United Democratic Front (UDF), which would coordinate antiapartheid protests within the country. Mandela was named a patron. The UDF campaigned successfully against the new parliament and grew into a powerful organization

Divide and rule

The three-chamber, or tricameral, parliament was a clever divide-and-rule ploy that separated black Africans from other ethnic groups but, by including Indians and Coloreds, appeared to show an easing of apartheid. The white population gave overwhelming support but, in 1984, more than 80 percent of eligible Indian and Colored voters boycotted elections to the new parliament.

that united more than 600 antiapartheid groups, including trade unions, community and church groups, and student associations. By the mid-1980s, the ANC was experiencing a massive revival. To Mandela's delight, it was the most popular political organization among black Africans, even though it had been banned for so long.

Further signs of international support came in 1984 when Bishop Desmond Tutu, a leading activist and supporter of nonviolent resistance, was awarded the Nobel Peace Prize. Mandela sent a letter of congratulation, but the authorities refused to deliver it.

◀ *A poster proclaims a meeting of the antiapartheid UDF in Cape Town, August 20, 1986.*

The Mandela "problem"

By 1985 calls for Mandela's release were universal. Botha was prepared to make some concessions, but not at the risk of lessening the power of the ruling minority. Mandela was now a big problem for the South African government. As a leading member of the ANC, a banned so-called terrorist organization, he could not be released by Botha without loss of face. Botha produced what he thought was a solution, publicly offering Mandela his freedom on condition that he would renounce violence. If Mandela refused, Botha could say the government was not standing in the way of his release.

It was not the first time the government had approached Mandela. As early as 1973 he had been offered freedom if he returned to Transkei, and by his reckoning he had received and rejected six conditional offers. Mandela had no intention of accepting this offer of release, but he also believed the time for negotiations with the government was fast approaching.

Mandela wrote to the foreign minister, Pik Botha, rejecting the offer. He prepared a public statement, which his daughter Zindzi read aloud to a cheering crowd. It was the first time Mandela's words had been heard in public for more than 20 years. In his statement, Mandela reaffirmed his loyalty to the ANC and called on Botha to renounce violence, dismantle apartheid, lift the ban on the ANC, and release the political prisoners. He reiterated his commitment to the people by stating: "I cannot and will not give any undertaking at a time when I and you, the people, are not free. Your freedom and mine cannot be separated."

Talking to the enemy

Some members of the government, including Kobie Coetsee, minister of justice, also knew negotiations were inevitable and that Mandela was the key. Following another hospital visit, Mandela was moved away from his comrades. The isolation gave him time to think, and he decided the time had come to talk to the government. He knew his ANC colleagues might not approve, but he felt if dialogue did not begin, South Africa would slide into civil war. He told no one of his plans, but wrote to Kobie Coetsee to propose talks. There was no reply.

In 1986 a British Commonwealth negotiating team, the Eminent Persons Group, came to Pollsmoor to see Mandela. Prison authorities made sure he was immaculately dressed. The prison commander told him he looked more like a prime minister than a prisoner. Mandela received the team with dignity and authority. He spoke about his views on an integrated society and reaffirmed his commitment to the Freedom Charter as the basis for a multiracial democratic South Africa. He also told them he favored the ANC entering negotiations with the government, but stressed that he spoke as an individual; only Tambo could speak for the ANC.

In 1987 a working group of senior South African government officials began conducting private talks with Mandela. He took these colleagues into his confidence, and over the next few years had many secret meetings with the Botha government.

Progress was slow, and while talks continued, the situation in South Africa deteriorated. In 1986 South Africa, under Botha's orders, launched an attack against ANC bases in Botswana, Zambia, and Zimbabwe. In response, Tambo and the ANC called for the people of South Africa to make the country ungovernable.

Winnie's role

Winnie Mandela took a high-profile role in the fight to free Mandela. As "Mother of the Nation" she was for many a world symbol of resistance to apartheid. But she was a controversial figure. In 1989 she was implicated in the kidnapping and murder of 14-year-old Stompie Moeketsi. She was later found guilty of kidnapping and faced further charges. For years Mandela believed in her innocence and felt his absence had caused her to go astray.

By the late 1980s the country was in turmoil. ANC bombing continued and state-initiated death squads targeted antiapartheid activists. In 1987 Mandela's house at 8115 Orlando West was burned down.

Although Tambo expressed reservations, Mandela continued to meet with government officials. He was even taken on secret trips outside the prison. There had been no pictures of Mandela for more than 20 years and no one recognized him. For the government there were critical issues in need of resolution, including the armed struggle and the ANC's alliance with the Communist Party. Mandela always referred his critics to the Freedom Charter.

Move to Victor Vorster

In 1988 Mandela was again admitted to the hospital with the early stages of tuberculosis, probably caused by years in damp cells. Afterward he was moved again, to a cottage within the grounds of Victor Vorster Prison. It was guarded and there was razor wire on the surrounding walls, but conditions were good. He had a cook and could receive unlimited visitors, including his family and political comrades from Robben Island and Pollsmoor. Even Sidelsky, his first employer, visited him. On Mandela's 71st birthday, most of his family came to celebrate. It gave him great pleasure, but also pain in knowing how many similar events he had missed over the years.

In 1989 the UDF formed an alliance with the Congress of South African Trade Unions (COSATU) to form the Mass Democratic Movement (MDM) and began organizing a countrywide civil disobedience campaign.

The beginning of the end

In 1989 Mandela finally met with P. W. Botha. It was a courteous meeting, but Botha refused Mandela's request to free political prisoners. In August Botha suddenly resigned and was succeeded by Frederik Willem de Klerk.

Despite being leader of the National Party, de Klerk was a realist. South Africa was politically isolated from the world. It was obvious that reform had to happen and black Africans would gain political rights, giving them majority rule. It was equally evident that Mandela and the ANC needed to play a part in the change. De Klerk stated his commitment to peace; he proved it when a mass demonstration against police brutality, led by Tutu, was given permission to proceed.

Events now moved fast. In October 1989 President de Klerk announced the unconditional release of Sisulu, Kathrada, and four Robben Island life prisoners. For Mandela, it was "a day we had yearned for and fought for over so many years."

Soon after, Mandela met with de Klerk and presented his conditions. He said apartheid could not be reformed, it had to be dismantled. There was no point in releasing him, he said, without unbanning the ANC and removing the causes of their struggle.

On February 2, 1990, in his opening speech to parliament, de Klerk said the time for negotiation had arrived.

He announced the lifting of bans on the ANC, PAC, the South African Communist Party and other liberation organizations, the end of press censorship, the release of some political prisoners, and the lifting of some emergency restrictions. He also gave notice that the apartheid laws would be repealed. Lastly, he announced that Mandela was to be released unconditionally and without delay.

It was the beginning of the end for apartheid. In Mandela's words: "One sweeping action had normalized South Africa. Our world changed overnight."

Mandela freed

Mandela's departure from prison was a hastily organized affair. On February 11 he was told he was to leave the next day. He protested that he needed time, but once he knew the world's press had been alerted, he made arrangements for Winnie and others to be flown in. At 4:00 P.M. on February 12, 1990, looking frail but dignified, he walked through the gates of Victor Vorster Prison, hand-in-hand with Winnie, a free man after 27 years.

▶ *The day everyone had been waiting for: Mandela walks from prison a free man, February 12, 1990.*

Mr. President

Mandela came out of prison to a huge welcome. His courage during his long imprisonment and his lack of bitterness impressed everyone, but there was still a long way to go. He was free but the institution was still in place. Apartheid had to be dismantled and a new constitution created.

Mandela faced a daunting task. South Africa had been deeply damaged by apartheid. The gap between wealth and poverty was enormous, and there was a legacy of bitterness in the country. Political groups were divided, there was violence in the townships, and in 1990 bitter fighting broke out in Natal between ANC supporters and Inkatha, the Zulu political movement headed by Chief Buthelezi. Mandela had to overcome distrust from those who felt he had made secret deals with the government as well as persuade de Klerk to accept a new constitution based on black majority rule.

There were personal problems, too. Winnie had taken a lover and the Stompie scandal soon reemerged; others followed. Mandela had missed Winnie desperately in prison, but their marriage was finished. In 1992 he separated from her, in 1996 they divorced.

Working toward change

Immediately after his release, Mandela went to Lusaka to persuade his old ANC comrades to enter negotiations with the government to end apartheid and introduce multiracial government. He was elected deputy president of the ANC.

He went on a tour of Europe and the United States to thank supporters. His intention was also to persuade western leaders to maintain economic sanctions against South Africa until negotiations were further advanced, and to raise funds for the ANC. He was greeted triumphantly wherever he went. Although he was 71, his energy and

▶ *From political prisoner to president: Mandela takes the oath as leader of the new South Africa.*

determination were remarkable. He attended functions and meetings, and did not always speak diplomatically. His support for Cuba's communist leader Fidel Castro, for instance, offended the American leadership.

Back in South Africa, he and some of his colleagues, including Sisulu, Slovo, and Kathrada, held their first meeting with de Klerk, who lifted the state of emergency. At first Mandela was not prepared to abandon armed struggle, but largely persuaded by Chris Hani, leader

of Umkhonto and a hero among young blacks, Mandela decided to suspend the armed struggle in August. Violence continued to escalate and Mandela sometimes had doubts about the decision. He believed (and it was later proven) that the state, using the security police, was joining in the violence to destabilize the townships. It made negotiations with the government extremely difficult.

To Mandela's great joy, Tambo returned to South Africa. The two old friends greeted each other like "boys on the

veldt" but Tambo was ill (he died in 1993). In 1991 Mandela was elected ANC president.

CODESA

In 1991 de Klerk repealed the remaining apartheid laws and serious talks began about the shape of an integrated South Africa. Negotiations between Mandela and de Klerk led to the formation of a Convention for a Democratic South Africa (CODESA) to work out a new constitution. It was a long and tortuous process and Mandela often lost patience with de Klerk. He was particularly frustrated by de Klerk's refusal to intervene and end the continuing violence in South Africa.

De Klerk was also concerned about safeguarding white minority influence in parliament under majority rule. Scandal began to undermine the government, which was implicated in widespread corruption and murder. In 1992 a referendum of white voters showed 69 percent in favor of a new constitution.

Negotiations often faltered, usually because of violence in the country. In 1992 more than 40 people were killed by Inkatha

◀ *A huge step forward: Mandela and F. W. de Klerk pose with their Nobel Peace Prize medals in 1993.*

in the black township of Boipatong, and in 1993 a white extremist assassinated Chris Hani. Mandela continued to apply pressure on de Klerk, but following Hani's death, he appealed for calm. In the midst of the scandals, Mandela was emerging as the country's next leader. Although some criticized him for being too authoritarian, his dignity, calm and commitment to reconciliation reassured most of the white electorate; the black population knew he had gone to prison for them.

In 1993 Mandela and de Klerk finally agreed on a timetable for the implementation of black majority rule. Following a request from Mandela, the United Nations lifted international economic sanctions. In October Mandela and de Klerk went to Oslo, where they were jointly awarded the Nobel Peace Prize for their work in ending apartheid. In December 1993 de Klerk's government settled on an interim constitution giving equal rights to all South Africans and abolishing the homelands.

Free elections

Elections were scheduled for April 1994. Only at the very last moment did Buthelezi and Inkatha agree to participate.

Mandela threw himself into the ANC campaign, traveling all over the country, greeted everywhere by huge crowds desperate to see the man they considered their hero. He loved campaigning, having lively discussions with journalists, shaking hands with everyone, and making long and involved speeches in stadiums and from open convertibles. He always dressed well and began wearing brightly colored silk shirts, which became his personal trademark.

The ANC issued a manifesto entitled *A Better Life for All*, which became its slogan. It committed the ANC to a program of new housing and jobs, free education, land redistribution, and many other social and economic reforms. It was a huge commitment, and Mandela warned his audiences that change would not happen overnight.

South Africa's first fully democratic elections began on April 28. Mandela cast his vote in a rural school in Inanda, Natal, where John Dube, founding president of the ANC, was buried. For Mandela it brought history full circle. Dube's mission, which had begun 82 years before, was about to be completed. As he voted, Mandela thought of his many

comrades who had died and could not be there. Mandela had a good sense of humor. When a journalist jokingly asked him who he would be voting for, Mandela replied, "You know, I have been agonizing over that choice all morning."

The elections lasted four days. South Africans voted in the millions, and enormous lines of people waited patiently for hours to cast their vote. For blacks it was the first time they had taken part in a democratic election, and some told Mandela they felt human at last. For whites the transition was a relief, and it felt as if the country had been reborn. Mandela found the mood buoyant. There were problems with misplaced ballots and rumors of fraud, but all went off smoothly and the country was more peaceful than it had been in years.

As expected the ANC won the election, with 62.6 percent of the vote. It did not have a two-thirds majority and so could not write the new constitution on its own. But Mandela was relieved. It meant other groups would have an input and the ANC could not be accused of

▶ *Thousands of people waited in line patiently for hours to vote in the 1994 elections.*

Rainbow nation

In the 1994 elections, the ANC won 62.6 percent of the vote, with 12.2 million mostly black votes, gaining 252 seats in the 400-seat National Assembly. The National Party won 20.4 percent, mainly white, Coloured, and Indian voters. Inkatha won 10.4 percent of the national vote and took control of the Kwa-Zulu-Natal provincial assembly. Afrikaner nationalists gained 425,000 votes, or 2.17 percent of the vote. The Democratic Party gained 1.7 percent of the vote, and the PAC 1.2 percent.

In Mandela's inaugural speech, he said: "We shall build the society in which all South Africans, both black and white, will be able to walk tall, without any fear in their hearts, assured of their inalienable right to human dignity—a rainbow nation at peace with itself and the world."

self-interest. At the victory celebrations Mandela, suffering from flu, thanked de Klerk, then took to the floor in a dignified solo dance. Nicknamed the "President's jive," it was copied in the townships and became another Mandela trademark.

Mandela was elected president on May 9, 1994. He was South Africa's first black president. It was a triumph for his long years of struggle and for the ANC. His inauguration was attended by more than 170 heads of state from all around the world.

The Presidency

In the spirit of reconciliation, Mandela promptly formed a government of national unity with the National Party. He appointed Thabo Mbeki, son of his comrade Govan Mbeki, first deputy president and de Klerk became second deputy president.

Mandela was 75 but he knew the struggle was not over yet. The minority white population controlled business and financial institutions, and the gaps in wealth between black and white were staggering. Whites made up only 13 percent of the population but earned 61 percent of its income. The average white income was eight times that of the average black income. Unemployment was over 30 percent and more than half the population lacked adequate housing, sanitation, clean water, electricity, and other basic facilities.

The ANC manifesto had promised great changes and the mood of the country was optimistic. But Mandela was cautious. Free health care was introduced for young children and pregnant mothers, but otherwise the pace of change was slow. Soon there were strikes for better pay and conditions.

Lawlessness continued in the townships and there were outbreaks of violent crime. Speaking in parliament, Mandela warned that riots and looting had to end and that the government did not have the money and resources to change South Africa overnight.

Despite the best of intentions, it was middle-class blacks who gained most from the immediate post-apartheid years. Although only about five percent of the black population, they gained access to the professional and business worlds that had been closed to them under apartheid, enjoying prosperity they had never known before. The economic gap among black Africans widened, and the fundamental problems of poverty would remain beyond Mandela's presidency.

Scandals and mistakes

Mandela's government was hit by some scandals, and he also made errors of judgement. He lived frugally but he and his ministers earned high salaries, which led to accusations of greed and an argument with Archbishop Desmond Tutu. Mandela, who donated a chunk of his earnings to a children's charity, eventually cut salaries, but the allegations had damaged his government. Between 1995 and 1997, some government ministers were accused of corruption and fraud, particularly misuse of aid money. Mandela did not always handle these matters well; he wanted to defend his colleagues, and accused others of trying to undermine the new government and its efforts.

Reconciliation

Mandela had greater success with his plans for forgiveness and reconciliation. He wanted to bring former opponents together, even setting up a reconciliation lunch to bring widows and wives of apartheid leaders together with those of leading black activists. Some critics accused Mandela of spending more time with whites than blacks, but his popularity in the opinion polls grew.

In 1995 he appointed a truth and reconciliation commission headed by Archbishop Tutu to document human rights abuses during apartheid and invite people to give evidence without danger of prosecution. More than 20,000 people came forward, and the report was completed in 1998. Evidence came to light of state involvement in the Inkatha violence and, in 1996, the National Party left the government.

Mandela also worked hard to reintegrate post-apartheid South Africa into the world community. He traveled abroad but also invited world leaders to visit him. As always, he remained even-handed. In 1998 both U.S. President Bill Clinton and Cuban leader Fidel Castro visited the country.

Retirement

Early in his presidency, Mandela said he would not seek a second term of office. He felt someone younger should take on the responsibility. He favored Thabo Mbeki as a successor and began to prepare for retirement. He had become friends with Graca Machel, widow of the former leader of Mozambique, and in 1998 they married. In 1999, at age 81, he retired from politics and with his new wife went to live in a country house that he had built in Qunu, the beloved village of his childhood. Mbeki became president.

Since retirement, Mandela spends most of his time in Qunu doing the things he missed while he was in prison, such as spending time with his large family. He also enjoys reading and following sporting events. Although no longer in politics, he remains a highly regarded statesman who continues to take an active interest in his country and the world.

South Africa still has problems, including unemployment, poverty, and AIDS. The society Mandela wanted has not yet been achieved, but his legacy is a democratic, integrated, and more stable country than anyone might have believed possible.

In Mandela's own words

"I have walked the long road to freedom. But I have discovered that after climbing a great hill, one only finds that there are many more hills to climb. I have taken a moment here to rest, to steal a view of the glorious vista that surrounds me, to look back on the distance I have come. But I can only rest for a moment, for with freedom come responsibilities, and I dare not linger, for my long walk is not yet ended."

▶ *Nelson Mandela and new wife Graca Machel acknowledge the crowds of well-wishers at Mandela's 80th birthday party, held on July 19, 1998.*

Glossary

African National Congress (ANC)
First black national organization in South Africa to campaign for African rights. Founded in 1912, it had regional or district congresses such as the Transvaal ANC. Banned between 1960 and 1990, it won the first integrated elections in 1994. The ANC worked with other liberation groups but did not allow white members.

African National Congress Youth League (ANCYL) Organization formed by Mandela, Sisulu, Tambo, and others and formally launched in 1944. Its radical policies were adopted by the ANC in 1949.

Afrikaans Simplified form of Dutch combined with Portuguese and African words. Dutch Afrikaans speakers were called Afrikaners.

Apartheid Afrikaans word meaning "apartness" or "separateness." It describes the legal system in South Africa between 1948 and 1991 that deliberately kept whites and nonwhites separate.

Bail Sum of money put up as security to make sure a released prisoner returns for trial. Mandela noted that, under apartheid, bail was on a sliding scale, the highest level of bail being for whites, middle for Indians, and the smallest bail for Africans and Coloreds.

Banning Apartheid measure forbidding someone from attending public gatherings of any kind, meeting groups of people, or having their words published. Mandela described it as "a kind of walking imprisonment."

Bantu Large group of related African languages spoken widely in central and southern Africa, including Xhosa and Zulu. Bantu literally means "people." The apartheid government used Bantu to mean African. The word is rarely used in South Africa today because of its apartheid connotations.

Bantustans So-called "black homelands" created under apartheid. Also known as Black National States. The South African government aimed to create black self-determining "nations" that would consequently deprive South Africans of citizenship.

Boer Dutch word meaning "farmer" and the name that Dutch settlers gave to themselves.

Boycott To refuse to use, buy, trade, or take part. During the apartheid years, many people outside South Africa refused to buy South African goods as part of the antiapartheid protest. Within the country, Africans boycotted European-only goods and services.

Censor To remove material not considered appropriate. Under apartheid, prison authorities censored letters to and from political prisoners.

Coloureds One of the racial groupings imposed by the apartheid regime. Coloureds, who lived mainly in the Cape, were people usually of mixed African and European origin.

Communism Political philosophy that believes that class or social grouping is the basis of oppression. Communists are people who follow communism. They believe revolution is needed to overthrow the upper classes and liberate the working classes and that land and industry should be owned by the state for the people.

Congress of Democrats White political group that supported the fight for democracy.

Congress of the People Also known as the Congress Alliance. An alliance of some 200 liberation groups including the ANC, the Indian Congress, the Congress of Democrats, church groups, and the Coloured People's Organization.

Democracy A political system in which everyone has the right to vote, regardless of race or gender. Representative or parliamentary democracy is the democratic system whereby people vote for their representatives in government.

Frontline states African nations in the "frontline" of the struggle against apartheid. They included Mozambique, Angola, Botswana, Lesotho, and Zimbabwe.

Homelands See Bantustans.

House arrest When a person is put under arrest but confined to his or her home rather than prison. It is illegal for that person to leave their home.

Imperialism Empire-building; the process whereby one nation extends its power over another by taking over territory and political and economic processes.

Indians One of the four racial groupings created by the apartheid regime. Most Indians were descendants of people from India who arrived in South Africa during the 1800s.

Kaffir A word used insultingly by Europeans, particularly Afrikaans speakers, to describe blacks in South Africa. Arabic in origin, it literally means "unbeliever."

Nationalism Belief that people who share a language or culture should be independent and achieve power for themselves.

National Party (NP) Afrikaner nationalist political party that introduced apartheid in 1948.

Pan African Congress (PAC) An African nationalist liberation group. Formed in 1959 as a breakaway group from the ANC, it was banned between 1960 and 1990.

Passbooks Under apartheid, a type of identity card or book that all blacks in South Africa had to carry by law. It showed where that person could live, work, and travel. Anyone not carrying a passbook could be arrested.

Radical Going to the root of a problem; someone who wants fundamental political change.

Sabotage To destroy buildings, machinery, or equipment deliberately in order to undermine or weaken an enemy.

Sanctions Actions taken by a country or countries against another to force change.

Segregation Separation. In apartheid South Africa, separation of different groups of people.

South African Indian Congress (SAIC)
Also, Indian Congress. Liberation organization formed by Indians in South Africa to fight for their rights.

State of Emergency Special measures such as increasing the military or police powers taken by the apartheid government to stay in power or maintain control.

Thembuland A province in Transkei.

Township Under apartheid, a poor area on the outskirts of a city where Africans were allowed to live.

Xhosa Related groups living mainly in the eastern Cape, South Africa. Part of the larger Nguni group of Bantu-speaking peoples.

Further Reading

Mandela, Nelson. *Mandela: An Illustrated Autobiography*. New York: Little, Brown, 1996.

Adi, Hokim. *Nelson Mandela: Father of Freedom*. Austin, Tex.: Raintree, 2001.

Gaines, Ann Graham. *Nelson Mandela and Apartheid in World History*. Berkeley Heights, N.J.: Enslow, 2001.

Holland, Gini. *Nelson Mandela*. Milwaukee: Gareth Stevens, 2002.

Mandela, Nelson. *Long Walk to Freedom: The Autobiography of Nelson Mandela*. New York: Little, Brown, 1995.

Sampson, Anthony. *Mandela—The Authorized Biography*. New York: Vintage, 2000.

Websites:
http://www.polity.org.za/people/mandela.html
http://www.anc.org.za/people/mandela.html

Time Line

circa 800 B.C. Khoisan peoples inhabit what is now South Africa.

100–300 A.D. Nguni, Tswana, and Sotho people begin to move into South Africa from the north.

1652 Dutch settlers arrive at the Cape.

1806 Britain takes over Cape Colony.

1820s King Shaka's Zulu warriors wage war.

1836 Boers begin their "Great Trek" from the Cape.

1870–80 British and Boer armies crush African kingdoms.

1880–81 First Anglo-Boer War.

1899–1902 Second Anglo-Boer War.

1906 Bambatha rebellion.

1910 Union of South Africa formed as a British dominion.

1912 ANC founded.

1913 Natives Land Act passed.

1918 Nelson Mandela born in Mvezo, Transkei.

1940 Mandela moves to Johannesburg.

1942 Mandela joins the ANC.

1944 Mandela and others launch ANC Youth League; Mandela marries first wife Evelyn Mase.

1948 National Party (NP) wins the election: apartheid becomes official government policy. Series of repressive laws introduced, including Population Registration Act (1949) and Group Areas Act (1950), separating different racial groups.

1950 Mandela is elected to ANC national executive committee.

1952 ANC launches Defiance Campaign; Mandela and Tambo open first black law firm in South Africa; Mandela elected president of Transvaal ANC; receives first banning order.

1953 Bantu Education Act provides inferior schooling for blacks.

1956 ANC adopts Freedom Charter; 20,000 women march in protest against pass laws.

1956–61 Treason Trial: 156 antiapartheid activists, including Mandela, stand trial for treason and are found not guilty.

1958 Mandela marries Nomzamo Winifred Madikizela (Winnie); they separate in 1992 and divorce in 1996.

1959 Pan African Congress (PAC) formed.

1960 Sharpeville massacre; ANC and PAC are banned.

1961 Mandela goes underground; becomes first commander of Umkhonto we Sizwe; armed struggle begins.

1962 Mandela secretly leaves South Africa; he is arrested on his return and imprisoned for five years; UN votes for sanctions against South Africa.

1963–64: Rivonia Trial: Mandela and other leaders sentenced to life imprisonment on Robben Island.

1970s black consciousness movement emerges in South Africa.

1976 Soweto uprising; police fire on schoolchildren.

1977 Steve Biko dies in police custody.

1980 "Free Mandela" campaign begins.

1981 South African government launches military force against ANC offices in Mozambique.

1982 Mandela is moved to Pollsmoor Prison on the mainland.

1983 United Democratic Front (UDF) formed.

1985 Countrywide uprising against apartheid. State of emergency declared; continues until 1990.

1987 Mandela begins series of secret talks with the South African government.

1988 Mandela is moved to Victor Vorster Prison.

1989 Walter Sisulu and five other political prisoners released unconditionally.

1990 President F. W. de Klerk legalizes the ANC, PAC, and other political groups and announces new constitution will be introduced. Mandela freed after 27 years in prison.

1991 Mandela is elected president of the ANC.

1993 Mandela and de Klerk awarded the Nobel Peace Prize.

1994 ANC wins first democratic election; Mandela becomes president of South Africa.

1998 Mandela marries Graca Machel.

1999 Mandela retires.

2002 Mandela expresses public concern about handling of AIDS crisis in South Africa.

Index

References shown in italic are pictures or maps.